# SHEET PAN SUPPERS

## Meatless

**100 Surprising Vegetarian Meals Straight from the Oven**

### RAQUEL PELZEL

WORKMAN PUBLISHING · NEW YORK

Library of Congress Cataloging-in-Publication Data is available.

ISBN: 978-0-7611-8993-0

Design by Becky Terhune
Photography by Ken Carlson, Waterbury Publications, Inc., Des Moines, IA
Food styling by Sue Moss, Main Dish Media
Author photograph by Evan Sung

Workman books are available at special discounts when purchased in bulk
for premiums and sales promotions as well as for fund-raising or educational
use. Special editions or book excerpts can also be created to specification.
For details, contact the Special Sales Director at the address below,
or send an email to specialmarkets@workman.com.

Workman Publishing Co., Inc.
225 Varick Street
New York, NY 10014-4381
workman.com

WORKMAN is a registered trademark of Workman Publishing Co., Inc.

Printed in China
First printing August 2017

10 9 8 7 6 5 4 3 2 1

To my boys, Julian and Rhys:
Yes, it was cooked on a sheet pan.

# Acknowledgments

**T**o my family of friends who keep me laughing and honest, whose shoulders I cry on, whose hands I hold, whose smiles make me warm all over, and who feed me when I need a warm meal and soulful nourishment—I love you all. You're the strong and nasty women who keep me inspired and hopeful: Lauren Sayre, Billie Dionne, Stacey Burrack-Watson, Adeena Sussman, Sara Kate Gillingham, Debbie Fiore-Manka, Jennifer Pahati-Kawa, Izabela Wojcik, Sabine Hrechdakian, Sandi Campo.

To my Workman family: Kylie Foxx McDonald, my editor, thanks for bringing me this book—it really tested my creativity and renewed my commitment to eating more plant-based foods for health and environmental wellness. I appreciate you letting me have my way with the concept. . . . Who ever thought I'd be making vegan poutine on a sheet pan?!? Becky Terhune and Anne Kerman, thanks for your artistic guidance, perseverance, and perspective. Selina Meere, Moira Kerrigan, and Chloe Puton, thank you for your enthusiasm, ideas, and positivity! Finally, to Carolan Workman and Susan Bolotin, thank you for creating a home for authors where we can explore and be creative and still (fingers crossed) sell lots of books!

To Ken Carlson and Sue Hoss (and Cinda Shambaugh), thanks for your focus, spirit, and kindness and making the recipes look as gorgeous as they taste. Go DSM!

To my agents, Sarah Smith and David Black: I always feel more sure-footed moving forward knowing you're both behind me. I couldn't ask for more supportive agents.

Marlon: You made this book better in every way.

To the readers who need to get dinner done: I hope this book brings your family together to share deliciously healthy and relatively straightforward meals that have a low impact on the environment and high impact on your well-being. Thanks for trusting my recipes, for investing your time and money to make them, and for giving them a seat at your table. I hope some of them get repeat invites and become frequent guests!

# Contents

# Introduction

## SHEET PAN SUPPERS: SIMPLE. VERSATILE. DELICIOUS.

**A**s a professional cook and recipe writer, I have a kitchen that's pretty tricked out with gadgets, pots, pans, and appliances. I have every tool you might need, from a cherry pitter to an at-home smoking gun, from humble one-fried-egg–size cast-iron skillets to the finest French-made copper potato steamer. But pop your head into my kitchen on a random Tuesday night, and you know what you'll see (at least three times out of four)? Me, cooking dinner on my beat-up and well-seasoned sheet pan. From broccoli to lasagna, couscous to soup (yes, soup!), a sheet pan is infinitely versatile and really—along with a wooden spoon and a sharp knife—all you need (besides an oven) to cook a dizzying collection of healthy and delicious meals.

Why? Because cooking on a sheet pan is *easy*. After a long day of writing and working on recipes, the last thing I want to do is make a giant mess in my kitchen. Just like you, I want to get a tasty and healthy meal on the table with as little fuss and drama as possible. I don't want to worry about something overcooking in a split second on the stovetop while I help one of my kids with homework or get distracted by a text message. Unless you're using the broiler (and then you do need to watch your food like a hawk so it doesn't burn, which *can* happen in a flash) or baking cookies or a cake, cooking on a sheet pan is generally a very forgiving method. Five more minutes on roasted cauliflower isn't going to destroy it—in fact, that extra time may make it that much more caramelized and golden-brown delicious.

Since my stovetop is free and clear, I don't have to worry about wiping it down from the grease splatters or drips and dribbles that happen while cooking. Like a skillet or frying pan, a sheet pan can be preheated in the oven to get a good sear on vegetables and tofu. If it's just me for lunch, I can use a quarter sheet; for me and my boys, I can use a larger pan, like a jelly roll pan; if I have a few friends joining us, then I can use a larger half sheet pan (see page xi for more on sizes) . . . or use two pans simultaneously in the oven. The best part is that sheet pans are inexpensive, with the average model costing about twenty bucks. It almost makes me question why I bother with any other pots and pans in the kitchen!

In my home I cook with veggies and plant-based proteins front and center. I'm not a vegetarian (though I was one—and went to a vegetarian cooking school—for several years), but 90 percent of the time I cook like one. Tofu, beans, lots of grains, and, of course, just about any and every colorful, tasty vegetable you

can imagine comes in and out of my fridge. My two sons have been eating this way since they were babies, so both are used to digging into a bowlful of sweet and spicy Hoisin Eggplant, Spicy Brussels Sprouts, and Tofu (page 59) or Crispy Roasted Shallot and Lentil Mujadara (page 133; see opposite page for suggestions on helping kids get down with their veggies). And really, it just makes sense to me from a sustainability perspective: Less water, less land, and fewer resources are used to grow a cabbage than raise a cow. The truth is that if we all ate less meat, the planet would be in a better place. I'm not going to get into statistics, but between water usage, carbon footprints, and the consumption of natural resources, you just can't beat a plant-forward diet for your own health and for the health of the planet.

When eating a vegetable-focused diet, it's very important to make sure you're eating diverse foods that deliver the nutrients you need. Beans and legumes are key for their protein and mineral content; leafy greens, cabbages, and colorful vegetables for vitamins and fiber; whole grains for fiber, complex carbohydrates, and satiety. There are chapters devoted to each in this book. But, that said, you don't have to "give up" on flavor or deliciousness when meat is removed from a recipe—this is by no means a "diet" book. On the contrary, I hope you find so much decadence and deliciousness in the recipes on these pages that you never miss the meat—or, if meat isn't part of your life, you find new ways to be satisfied, all by what is roasted, braised, steamed, slow-cooked, and stewed on a humble sheet pan.

There are a few things to consider when buying a sheet pan. Number-one consideration: size. The largest one I have is a 13 x 18-inch pan, also called a half sheet. This is your kitchen workhorse, the sheet pan you *must* have. Though sheet pans come in full sizes (18 x 26 inches), unless you have a restaurant-size range, a pan that big won't fit in your oven. A half sheet pan is what you need for baking cookies or

## Kids and Vegetables: How to Make Nice

So you say your kid won't eat broccoli. Or Brussels sprouts. Or cauliflower or cabbage or bell peppers or onions, and did I mention mushrooms? The key to getting kids to eat their vegetables is to force them. No, of course not—I joke! Really, though, in all seriousness, having a picky eater can make mealtimes stressful, to say the least, and even embarrassing if you have friends over and your child throws a tantrum over the peas on his or her plate.

What I have learned by raising two boys who love vegetables (not all vegetables, but most) is this: Persistence pays; guilt, pleading, and bribery do not. Our house rule is that you have to try one bite of everything. You don't have to like it, you don't have to take more, but you have to try it, because if you don't try, you just never know. You could be missing out on your new favorite food (Jerusalem artichokes . . . who knew?).

Of course, the easiest way to get your kids to try new things is always to have familiar options surrounding the newbie. Offer something simple (buttered noodles) with an entry-level vegetable (salted celery sticks or cucumbers splattered with soy sauce) alongside a semi-challenging dish (Spiced Carrot Salad with Creamy Basil Dressing, page 40) and/or one wild card (Tofu Puttanesca with Garlic Bread, page 81). That way, you're guaranteed your kids will eat something and you know they'll at least try the carrots and the tofu. If they don't like it, there's no fighting or bribing. They can happily eat the noodles and the cucumbers and feel proud for trying the new items. And you know what? The next time you serve one of those "new" items, it won't be totally unfamiliar, which means—maybe—your kids will be less hesitant to take a bite . . . and maybe even like it. Win-win all around.

biscuits, making soup or stew, or roasting pretty much anything in this book. What a half sheet pan doesn't work for is baking a cake or making banana bread—unless you want to double the batch and bake enough for twenty!

In addition to the half sheet pan, I'm a big fan of the jelly roll pan—and urge you to get one (they're cheap) if you don't already have one. These come in different sizes—mine is 10 x 15 inches. This is the perfect size for baking cakes and making bar cookies and is what I used to develop all the recipes in the dessert chapter (see page 207). Of course, you can roast smaller portions of vegetables or toast nuts or bread crumbs on it, too.

*You can use any size sheet pan for the recipes in this book—unless a specific size is called for. But by and large, any size will work.*

The smallest size I have is a quarter sheet pan. This is a 9 x 13-inch pan. I use it to toast bread or nuts, make a frittata for two, or bake a single galette or just a few cookies. But that's about it. If there was one sheet pan to skip, this would be it (sorry, quarter sheet!).

It's important that your sheet pan feels sturdy when you pick it up. If it feels flimsy, chances are it will permanently warp when you heat it for searing vegetables. Nearly all sheet pans warp a little when preheated and have cold items added to them (you may even hear your sheet pan "pop" in the oven), but low-quality ones won't return to normal—they'll stay twisted and rounded in odd places.

Generally, most sheet pans have rim heights around $7/8$ to 1 inch. This is important *especially* when making rice or a hot stew because you add liquid to the sheet pan and you want to make sure your sheet pan can contain that liquid.

The finish of a sheet pan makes a difference, too—see page 208 for a more in-depth explanation of how a dark finish can affect your baking or the brownness of roasted vegetables. I also prefer a smooth-bottomed sheet pan to one with ridges or a textured finish, which are tough to clean.

Additionally, I prefer a traditional pan to a nonstick one. Nonstick coating makes it more difficult for food to caramelize and develop *fond*, the flavorful browned bits on the bottom of a pan that accumulate during browning and roasting. After adding liquid to a pan once fond has formed, you stir it to incorporate the fond into the sauce—it's like liquid gold! Why would you want to avoid it? Besides, most burnt bits come off a sheet pan with a simple soapy soak in the sink. (For super-burnt corners, I'll boil water, pour it in, and use a steel wool scrubbie on it to give it a really good once-over.) If you use a liner—be it aluminum foil, parchment paper, or a silicone mat (I love these for baking!)—you'll avoid sticky pan situations altogether.

## GETTING THE BEST RESULTS: READ, NOTE, AND NOTICE

Being a good cook is partly about knowing how flavors come together, partly about technique and process, and the rest is really about discipline: reading a recipe from top to bottom *before* you start cooking, getting your ingredients together and prepped before you begin, and making any notes in the recipe to help you cook smarter and faster. (For example, I sometimes make brackets around ingredients that can be combined in one bowl to help cut down on dirty dishes.)

This is all in an effort to anticipate what might happen as you cook and reduce the possibility of getting flustered because you forgot to mince the garlic or measure one cup of canned coconut milk. Being less stressed in the kitchen means you'll have more fun, and having more fun will, hopefully, encourage you to get into the kitchen and cook more often.

Recipes are great, but the reason all our grandmas make the best this and that is because they've had more than fifty years to practice!

Practice makes perfect, especially when it comes to cooking.

Being aware in your kitchen is also key to being a good, smart, and efficient cook. Noticing if your oven has hot spots (meaning you'll have to rotate the baking sheet to avoid burnt areas) or whether your oven runs hot or cold (invest in a basic oven thermometer to know for sure) is really important when it comes to cooking times and not burning food. To be extra safe, I always, *always* set the timer for five minutes before the recipe indicates the food will be done—that allows me to catch a hot oven before it ruins a cake or gives me an opportunity to jack up the temperature if whatever I'm cooking is moving too slowly. Everyone's oven runs at a different temperature, everyone's broiler is different. A recipe is a road map but you're the driver—you're always the one in control.

There are so many ways to simplify your dinner routine, whether you're cooking on a sheet pan, in a skillet, or a soup pot: rinsing, trimming, and chopping onions, carrots, peppers, and other nonperishable items when you get home with them from the market (never wash herbs or tender greens until just before using); prepping your vegetables in advance (like while you're waiting for coffee to brew in the morning) and bagging them in resealable

## Hi, Vegan and Gluten-Free Friends!

If a recipe is marked **V** , that means it's suitable for our vegan pals, those who choose not to include any animal products in their diet (including dairy, eggs, and honey). Often, even if a recipe is not specifically tagged as vegan, it can be made vegan with an easy honey/maple syrup swap, or exchanging dairy milk cheese for vegan cheese (these recipes are marked **VO** for "vegan optional"). Nearly half the recipes in this book are vegan.

If you're gluten sensitive or have celiac disease, you can make nearly half the recipes in this book straight up, or, with some swaps (like using gluten-free bread crumbs, or shoyu in place of soy sauce) you can make even more of the recipes. Recipes that are gluten free are marked with **GF**; there are forty-eight of these—almost half.

For a full rundown of which recipes are vegan, vegan optional, and/or gluten free, refer to the table of contents on page v.

bags (rinse and reuse them after!) or airtight containers; measuring dry ingredients for a coffee cake or granola the night before you want to make it; or even just lining up the spices and any pantry items on your counter in the morning so when you get home, everything is ready to go. I know what it's like to get home after seven at night and be starving but have no energy and no drive to cook (and cleanup afterward? Forget it!).

Just about any recipe in this book that is not in the dessert chapter (see page 207) can stand alone as dinner (though depending on your hunger level, you may want to cook some sheet pan grains on the side; see page 87). I've considered protein, carbohydrates, and satiety—you know, that great feeling of being full and happy. That said, you can always pair two sheet pan recipes and cook them side by side as long as the temperatures in the instructions match.

I hope this book offers you lots of ideas and options so you always feel inspired to make a home-cooked meal. Whether you're a vegetarian, or vegan, or just want to get your family to eat a greener diet a few times a week, may the sheet pan help you get there.

Chapter 1

# BITS, BITES, AND SNACKS

Okay, I'm not your mother. I'm not going to tell you *not* to eat potato skins or nachos or caramelized onion dip for dinner because—you know what? I sure have! So even though this is technically the snack chapter, you can absolutely turn Babaghanouj (page 18) into a meal with some pita and roasted vegetables, or make a small garden salad to serve with Roasted Pepper, Olive, and Feta Burekas (page 13) or an Any-Way-You-Like Veggie Turnovers (page 8). The Super Seedy Power Bars (page 25) are definitely satisfying and wholesome enough to be a meal on their own (especially for a power breakfast). Add some steamed rice and a cucumber-tomato salad to the Oven-Roasted Okra Chips with Dill Pickle Dip (page 22) and there you have it—dinner. And I have been known to add kale chips (page 23) to pesto to add a savory boost. So here you go—a snack chapter that defies titles and refuses to limit its potential to between-meal consumption.

# BBT BITES

B lue cheese, basil, tomatoes . . . I mean YUM. With a little smoky salt and the crunch of toasted baguette slices, this is perfection on bread. Here I turn the blue cheese into a thick dressing that gets spooned over a basil leaf (instead of lettuce). A tomato slice goes on top, nearly concealing the blue cheese so when you bite in it's a total explosion of flavor. Use heirloom tomatoes when they're available, preferably in a multitude of hues to brighten your platter and make you smile. (They always make me smile.)

If making these for a party, I often triple the blue cheese dressing and chop some raw veggies to put alongside it. Can you ever have too much blue cheese dip on hand? I didn't think so.

---

½ cup crumbled blue cheese

3 tablespoons buttermilk, plus extra as needed (see Note)

3 to 4 tablespoons mayonnaise

2 teaspoons fresh lemon juice, plus extra as needed

About 1 teaspoon pickle juice, plus extra as needed (if you have a jar in the fridge; optional)

1½ teaspoons smoked salt (preferably a flaky sea salt like smoked Maldon), plus extra as needed (see box, page 4)

½ teaspoon freshly ground black pepper, plus extra for serving

1 baguette, sliced into ¼- to ½-inch-thick slices on a diagonal

2 garlic cloves, halved lengthwise

3 tablespoons extra-virgin olive oil

16 large fresh basil leaves

3 very juicy, ripe tomatoes (about ¾ pound), sliced to fit the bread (you want 16 slices)

---

1. Stir together the blue cheese, 3 tablespoons buttermilk, 3 tablespoons mayonnaise, lemon juice, pickle juice (if using), ½ teaspoon salt, and pepper in a medium-size bowl. The dressing should be on the thick side; add the remaining mayonnaise if needed to make it thicker. Taste and add another tablespoon buttermilk and more lemon juice, pickle juice, or salt if needed. Cover the bowl with plastic wrap and refrigerate until serving (or for up to 5 days).

2. Adjust an oven rack to the upper-middle position and preheat the broiler to high. Lay the baguette slices on a sheet pan. Rub each slice with the cut side of a garlic clove half. Dip a pastry brush or silicone brush into the olive oil and dab it over the bread. Sprinkle with smoked salt.

3. Toast the baguette slices until they are golden brown, 3 to 4 minutes (watch the bread closely as broiler intensities vary). Turn the slices and return the pan to the oven. Toast on the other side until the bread feels dry but isn't yet golden, 1 to 2 minutes. (You don't want the bread to get golden because it will be too crunchy! Better to have one browned side and one not-so-crisp side so your guests can bite in easily.)

4. Remove the toast from the oven and set it aside to cool for 5 minutes. Lay a basil leaf on each piece of toast so it rests on it like a little cup. Spoon a little blue cheese dressing into the basil leaf and place a tomato slice on top. Sprinkle with more salt and pepper and serve.

NOTE: If you don't have buttermilk on hand, combine 2½ tablespoons milk with 1½ teaspoons fresh lemon juice and use in its place.

## Get Your Smoke On

A little smoky essence brings a whole new dimension of flavor and captivation to food. Smoked paprika (pimenton) and smoked salt and pepper are pretty widely available in grocery stores and specialty markets. You can even find smoked soy sauce and smoked sesame seeds in some gourmet shops. Lapsang Souchong tea, a smoky black tea, is also wonderful for using in brines (brew the tea) or herby rubs, (pulverize the dry tea with other herbs and spices—this is great as a brine or rub for tofu or as a rub for eggplant or beets). You can even place vegetables on a wire rack, add brewed Lapsang Souchong tea to the sheet pan, cover everything tightly with aluminum foil, and roast the vegetables in a hot oven for a little smokehouse situation. Or try adding soaked wood smoking chips to the bottom of a sheet pan (enclose the chips in an aluminum foil pack with a few holes poked into it to release smoke), place a wire rack on top, and set the food to be smoked on top of the rack, and then roast in a hot oven. From tomatoes to carrots, indoor smoking is a fun way to put your sheet pan to work.

# CHILI NACHOS

*SERVES 4*

When my kids have had a particularly hard week, I tell them we're having nachos for dinner. Just like that, the sky is blue again! Though nachos may seem like "junk" food, they are actually not *that* bad for dinner—especially when you top them with a protein- and fiber-packed heap of beans, fresh corn, and veggie crumbles (find them in the freezer section of the grocery store near the veggie burgers). Happy kids make for a happy mom. And sometimes I even make nachos when they're *not* home—but that's just between you and me.

---

1 bag (8 ounces) tortilla chips
1 cup veggie crumbles (such as Beyond Meat's Beyond Beef Beefy Crumbles)
2 ears fresh corn, husked, kernels sliced off the cob, or 1 cup frozen corn
1 can (15 ounces) black beans or pinto beans, drained and rinsed
½ cup canned crushed tomatoes
1 teaspoon chili powder
¼ teaspoon cayenne pepper (optional)

2 cups shredded mild Cheddar cheese
1 cup shredded mozzarella cheese
½ cup crumbled Cotija cheese
½ cup finely chopped fresh cilantro leaves
Charred Tomatillo Salsa (page 16) or your favorite store-bought salsa, for serving
Pickled jalapeño chiles, for serving (optional)
Sour cream, for serving (optional)

---

1. Adjust an oven rack to the upper-middle position and preheat the oven to 400°F.

2. Spread the tortilla chips in a single layer on a rimmed sheet pan.

3. Combine the veggie crumbles, corn, beans, tomatoes, chili powder, and cayenne (if using) in a large bowl and stir together with a wooden spoon. Use the spoon to dollop and spread the mixture over the chips. Sprinkle with the shredded Cheddar and mozzarella cheeses.

4. Bake the nachos until the cheeses melt and begin to bubble and become golden in spots, 6 to 8 minutes. Turn the broiler to high and continue to cook the nachos until the cheeses are browned and molten-bubbly, about 2 minutes more (watch the chips closely as broiler intensities vary).

5. Remove the nachos from the oven and set the pan on a large trivet—tell your guests the pan is hot! (I like to fold 2 hand towels around each side of the pan to remind people not to touch.) Sprinkle the Cotija and cilantro over the nachos and serve with the salsa, pickled jalapeños (if using), and sour cream (if using).

# ANY-WAY-YOU-LIKE VEGGIE TURNOVERS

*MAKES 10 TURNOVERS*

The flavor of the roasted vegetables in these flaky turnovers is sweet and earthy, the portobello mushrooms offering their meaty taste while the scallion and garlic keep things bright and interesting. I've added spicy-herby Jamaican jerk seasoning, curry powder, garam masala, herbes de Provence, and Chinese five-spice powder to the vegetable filling (and switched up the veggies accordingly—see box, page 10 for suggestions) . . . Depending on the blend you add, the turnovers take on a different global tone.

For speed and ease, I use store-bought piecrust dough, but when I'm making these for a party or special occasion, you bet they're being stuffed into homemade dough. If you make homemade dough for these, use a recipe that makes enough for a double deep-dish piecrust. If you like your turnovers on the extra flaky side, use puff pastry instead.

3 scallions, ends trimmed, very finely chopped

2 garlic cloves, minced

1 medium-size portobello mushroom or 5 cremini mushrooms, stemmed and very finely chopped

1 small green bell pepper, stemmed, seeded, and very finely chopped

1 small red bell pepper, stemmed, seeded, and very finely chopped

1 small tomato, cored and very finely chopped

2 teaspoons jerk seasoning or spice blend of choice (such as curry powder, garam masala, ras el hanout, za'atar, Italian seasoning blend, Chinese five-spice powder, or herbes de Provence)

1 tablespoon finely chopped fresh thyme leaves

1 teaspoon ground turmeric (omit it if using a Mediterranean spice blend)

1 teaspoon plus a pinch of kosher salt

½ teaspoon freshly ground black pepper

2 tablespoons extra-virgin olive oil

¼ cup finely chopped fresh cilantro leaves

8 ounces piecrust dough, store-bought or homemade, or thawed frozen puff pastry

1. Adjust an oven rack to the middle position and preheat the oven to 375°F. Line a rimmed sheet pan with parchment paper or aluminum foil.

2. Stir together the scallions, garlic, mushroom, green and red bell peppers, tomato, jerk seasoning, thyme, turmeric, salt, pepper, and olive oil in a medium-size bowl and turn them out onto the prepared sheet pan.

3. Roast the vegetables until the tomatoes are very soft and have released all their liquid, stirring midway through cooking, about 20 minutes. Transfer the vegetables to a fine-mesh sieve set over a large bowl and let them cool and drain. (Don't press on the vegetables; just let gravity do the work.) Transfer to a small bowl and stir in the cilantro. Line the sheet pan with a fresh sheet of parchment paper.

4. Roll the dough (if it isn't rolled already) between 2 sheets of parchment paper or plastic wrap into a ¼- to ⅛-inch-thick disk. With a 4- or 4½-inch biscuit cutter (or upside-down bowl or plastic container lid), stamp out as many dough circles as close together as possible. Transfer the circles to the prepared sheet pan with a spatula. Gently gather the scraps together, press them flat, re-roll as instructed previously, and cut out as many circles as possible. Discard any remaining scraps. You should get about 20 circles.

5. Scoop 1 heaping tablespoon of vegetables onto the bottom third of each dough circle, leaving a ½-inch edge of dough. Fold the top of the circle over the bottom to enclose the vegetables, pressing the edges together to seal the seam, then pressing the tines of a fork around the seam to make a decorative edge. Freeze the turnovers for 15 minutes or refrigerate them for 30 minutes to chill the dough.

6. Bake the turnovers until golden brown, 20 to 24 minutes. Remove from the oven and cool for 5 minutes before transferring to a wire rack to cool completely. Serve warm or cool. The turnovers will keep, in an airtight container at room temperature, for up to 2 days.

## Spice and Vegetable Combos

The vegetables in the Any-Way-You-Like Veggie Turnovers (page 8) come together to create a flavor that works beautifully as a foundation for any number of seasonings. Here are some ideas for spice blends and potential veggie additions to give your turnovers that extra note of uniqueness.

Keep the tomatoes and red bell pepper but, instead of the portobello mushrooms and green bell pepper, substitute the following:

| PAIR THIS . . . | WITH THAT |
| --- | --- |
| Very finely chopped shiitakes and snow peas | Chinese five-spice powder |
| Whole peas and very finely chopped carrots | Garam masala |
| Very finely chopped eggplant and fennel | Herbes de Provence |
| Very finely chopped potatoes and whole peas | Indian curry powder |
| Very finely chopped fennel and portobellos | Italian seasoning blend |
| Shredded coconut and chopped spinach | Jamaican curry powder |
| Smashed chickpeas and chopped fresh mint | Ras el hanout |
| Smashed chickpeas and very finely chopped eggplant | Za'atar |

# CHEESY STUFFED POTATO SKINS

(GF) *MAKES 8 POTATO SKINS*

I used to order potato skins in burger joints, and they'd arrive on a diner-style plate, crispy edged from the fryer—yes, those hollowed shells are usually deep-fried before stuffing—and nearly molten because they were loaded with so much cheese. This version is somewhere between potato skins and a twice-baked potato. It's still indulgent and delicious, just a bit more fancy (as my eleven-year-old son would say) and a little healthier. This is a fantastic party hors d'oeuvre, by the way, made with halved small new potatoes hollowed and stuffed. So adorable!

---

4 medium-size Yukon Gold potatoes, halved lengthwise
2 tablespoons extra-virgin olive oil
5 tablespoons unsalted butter, melted
1 teaspoon kosher salt, plus extra as needed

½ teaspoon freshly ground black pepper
⅓ cup sour cream
½ cup shredded Cheddar cheese, plus extra for sprinkling
¼ cup shredded mozzarella cheese
2 tablespoons finely chopped fresh chives, plus extra for garnish

---

1. Adjust an oven rack to the middle position and preheat the oven to 350°F.

2. Slice off a thin sliver from each rounded side of the potato halves so they sit upright. Place the potatoes on a rimmed sheet pan and rub them all over with the olive oil. Set them cut side up and bake until a paring knife slips easily into the center of a potato meeting no resistance, about 45 minutes (if using baby potatoes, they will take about half as long).

3. Remove the potatoes from the oven and set aside to cool for 20 minutes. With a spoon, carefully scoop out the center of each potato half, leaving a ¼-inch border around the edge and a bit of potato in the bottom. Place the scooped potato in a medium-size bowl. Return the shells to the sheet pan, hollow side up.

4. Pour 4 tablespoons melted butter over the scooped potato in the bowl. Season with the salt and pepper. Mash until well combined. Stir in the sour cream, taste and add more salt

if needed. Stir in the Cheddar and mozzarella cheeses and the chives.

5. Adjust an oven rack to the upper-middle position and preheat the broiler to high. Dip a pastry brush or silicone brush into the remaining tablespoon melted butter and dab it over the tops of the potato shells on the sheet pan. Sprinkle a few pinches of salt over them and place the shells in the oven. Broil until the shells are golden brown, 4 to 8 minutes (watch them closely as broiler intensities vary). Remove from the oven and set aside. Leave the broiler on.

6. With a spoon, divide the potato filling among the shells, filling each completely without packing the potato mixture in too tightly. Sprinkle the tops of the potatoes with Cheddar cheese and place the sheet pan under the broiler until the potatoes sizzle and begin to get golden brown, 3 to 4 minutes (again watching closely to avoid burning). Remove the potatoes from the oven and serve hot, garnished with chives.

## More Potato Toppers

Instead of shredded Cheddar, mozzarella, and chives, try these topper combinations:

| FOR THE CHEDDAR | FOR THE MOZZARELLA | FOR THE CHIVES |
|---|---|---|
| Feta | Pecorino Romano | Finely chopped fresh scallions |
| Fontina | Parmigiano Reggiano | Finely chopped fresh basil |
| Fresh goat cheese | Blue cheese | Finely chopped fresh tarragon |
| Havarti | Aged Gouda | Finely chopped fresh dill |
| Pepper Jack | Cheddar | Finely chopped fresh cilantro |

# ROASTED PEPPER, OLIVE, AND FETA BUREKAS

MAKES 6 BUREKAS

There used to be this Israeli restaurant in Chicago where my dad held court with a bunch of other Israeli hotheads. They'd sit at the table closest to the kitchen and argue about politics, sports, and home remodeling and drink lots of coffee and order plates of hummus and babaghanouj, bowls of lentil soup, and always burekas, which are flaky turnovers stuffed with vegetables and, sometimes, cheese. They spoke in Hebrew; I couldn't understand a word, so I just quietly loaded my plate with all the good stuff and sat, minding my own business, deep diving into the deliciousness.

---

⅓ cup whole-milk ricotta
¼ cup crumbled feta cheese
3 tablespoons finely grated Pecorino Romano cheese
2 teaspoons roughly chopped fresh oregano, rosemary, or thyme leaves
¼ cup pitted black olives (preferably oil-cured), roughly chopped

1 teaspoon finely grated lemon zest
¼ teaspoon plus a pinch of kosher salt
1 large egg
1 cup roughly chopped roasted red bell peppers (jarred is fine)
1 sheet thawed frozen puff pastry
Flour, for rolling the puff pastry
Sesame seeds, for sprinkling

---

1. Adjust an oven rack to the middle position and preheat the oven to 400°F. Line a rimmed sheet pan with parchment paper or a silicone mat.

2. Whisk the ricotta, feta, Pecorino Romano, oregano, black olives, lemon zest, and ¼ teaspoon salt in a medium-size bowl. Crack the egg into a small bowl and lightly beat it. Add half the beaten egg and the roasted peppers to the cheese mixture and stir to combine. Into the remaining beaten egg, whisk 1 teaspoon water and a pinch of salt to make an egg wash (for sealing and brushing the top of the pastry).

3. Place the puff pastry on a lightly floured work surface and roll it to ⅛- to ¼-inch thickness. Cut the pastry horizontally down the middle, then cut vertically into thirds so you have 6 pieces. Depending on the size of your puff pastry sheet, you will have 6 squares or rectangles—it doesn't really matter. Spoon about ¼ cup of cheese filling onto the bottom third of each piece leaving a ½-inch border at the bottom. Dip a pastry brush into the egg wash and coat the bottom edges and sides with it. Fold the top of each pastry over the bottom to enclose the cheese filling, pressing to seal the edges. Transfer the burekas to the prepared sheet pan, brush the tops with egg wash, and sprinkle with sesame seeds.

4. Bake until the pastry is golden brown, 25 to 30 minutes. Remove from the oven and transfer to a wire rack to cool before serving. The burekas are best eaten fresh, within 1 hour of baking. If you want to make them ahead of time, rewarm them in a 300°F oven until they are warm and flaky again.

# CHARRED TOMATILLO SALSA

(V) (GF)  *MAKES ABOUT 3 CUPS*

I think I go through more tomatillo salsa than red salsa and pico de gallo combined. The acidity in it makes it a great topper or mix-in—have you ever tried guacamole with a spoonful or two of tomatillo salsa mixed in? It's a great snack-y dip, of course, but for a taco bar (see box, page 77), Loaded Chilaquiles with Baked Eggs (page 180), or even for saucing sheet pan–roasted tofu, tomatillo salsa is an absolute workhorse that takes barely a nod to make. You can also double the batch and freeze half because you will—without a doubt—become as addicted as I am. (It will keep, frozen, for up to 6 months.)

---

1½ pounds tomatillos, husked
   and rinsed under cold water
   (see box, page 17)
6 garlic cloves
2 medium-size poblano peppers
2 serrano or jalapeño chiles
   (jalapeños are milder, FYI)
1 tablespoon extra-virgin olive oil

2½ teaspoons kosher salt, plus extra
   as needed
1 cup packed fresh cilantro, including
   tender stems
1 tablespoon distilled white vinegar,
   plus extra as needed
Tortilla chips, for serving (optional)

---

1. Adjust an oven rack to the upper-middle position and preheat the broiler to high.

2. Place the tomatillos on a rimmed sheet pan with the garlic, poblanos, and serranos. Toss with the olive oil and 1 teaspoon salt. Turn the tomatillos stem-side up.

3. Broil until the tomatillos color a bit on top and the poblanos begin to char, about 15 minutes. With tongs, turn the poblanos; leave the tomatillos as they are. Continue to broil until the tops of the tomatillos are blackened and they have begun to pop and deflate, 5 to 8 minutes more (watch the tomatillos closely as broiler intensities vary). Remove the sheet pan from the oven.

4. Transfer the poblanos to a small bowl and cover the bowl with plastic wrap; scrape everything else into the bowl of a food processor (or use a blender). Set both aside to cool for 15 minutes.

5. Uncover the poblanos. With a paring knife, stem the peppers, slit them open lengthwise, and use the tip of the knife to remove the seeds. Peel the peppers (no need to be fastidious—just peel off any skin that comes off easily) and add them to the food processor.

6. Add the cilantro, vinegar, and remaining 1½ teaspoons salt. Process until the mixture is semi-smooth and the cilantro is very fine, about ten (1-second) pulses. Taste and season with more salt or vinegar if needed. Serve immediately with tortilla chips (if using) or refrigerate in an airtight container for up to 1 week.

## Oh, *That's* a Tomatillo

You know that bin of parchment paper–colored husk-covered green tomatoes at the market? Yeah, *those*. That's a tomatillo! They're wonderfully acidic and tart and make one heck of a good salsa. Look for tomatillos that are firm and taut beneath the husk (peel it back to peek just like you would with an ear of corn), not shriveled, soft, or bruised. Before using, peel off the papery skins and rinse the tomatillos under cold water to remove the sticky coating on the surface. Now you're good to go! In a pinch, you can use green tomatoes as a substitute (and by green I mean unripe tomatoes, not Green Zebra or other green-colored heirloom varietals).

# BABAGHANOUJ

Ⓥ ⒼⒻ *MAKES 1 3/4 CUPS (OR 1 1/4 CUPS IF STRAINED)*

**W**hen it comes to eggplant dip, I'm a bit of a *baba* snob—having an Israeli father will do that to you. When I was a kid, we traveled around to Chicago's Middle Eastern restaurants sampling babas made by expats from all over the region. In the end, our favorite didn't come from any one country in particular—the best tasting baba is always the freshest baba—usually one with a good amount of garlic and lemon juice (a smoky char doesn't hurt either). While you can buy prepared versions, once you taste homemade you will be spoiled forever.

---

2 large or 5 medium-size eggplants (about 2 pounds total)

⅓ cup tahini (sesame paste)

¼ cup ice water

2 tablespoons fresh lemon juice, plus extra as needed

2 garlic cloves, grated on a Microplane-style rasp

2 teaspoons kosher salt, plus extra as needed

Warm pita bread, crackers, or vegetable sticks (carrots, celery, or cucumbers), for serving

Ground sumac (see box, page 19; optional)

---

1. Adjust an oven rack to the middle position and preheat the oven to 425°F. Line a rimmed sheet pan with aluminum foil.

2. With a fork, prick one side of each eggplant 3 or 4 times. Place them on the prepared sheet pan and roast until they collapse completely and a paring knife inserted into the center meets no resistance, about 40 minutes.

3. Cut an X in the base of each eggplant. Stand them upright (with the X facing down) in a fine-mesh sieve set over a bowl to drain and

cool for 30 minutes. Discard the liquid that accumulates. Place each eggplant on a cutting board and, with a chef's knife, make a slit lengthwise from end to end, being careful not to cut all the way through. Open the eggplant like a book. Scoop out the flesh and chop it very, very finely, then place it in a large bowl.

4. Whisk in the tahini, ice water, lemon juice, garlic, and salt. Taste and adjust the seasoning with more salt or lemon juice if needed. For an extra silky babaghanouj, you can push the mixture through a fine-mesh sieve

to remove seeds and bits of flesh (but I like it rough and rustic).

5. Serve with the pita. The babaghanouj will keep, refrigerated in an airtight container, for a few days. Sprinkle with ground sumac (if using) right before serving.

## Say What? Say Sumac

In the Middle East, ground sumac, the dried, pulverized fuchsia berries from a shrub, is used as a finishing sprinkle to add tartness to a dish. It can be used in place of lemon juice for its sour taste and, as an added bonus, it adds a pretty hint of purple to whatever it is sprinkled on. You can find it in Middle Eastern markets and many spice shops and, of course, online.

# CARAMELIZED ONION DIP

GF   *SERVES 6*

Onion dip is the world's greatest icebreaker. A bowlful of this stuff is like a magnet at parties—friends can't resist it and everyone always ends up crowded around the bowl, sharing stories about onion dips (and parties) of their past. The savory-umami taste of the caramelized onion combined with the fresh, rich sour cream and the sharpness of chives is just a winner, plain and simple—and blows away anything sprinkled from a packet.

Caramelizing the onions on a sheet pan is a genius trick (if I do say so myself) that frees up your stovetop to do other things (or just stay clean for the party); of course, caramelized onions can be used in a million and one ways, from grilled cheese to topping a pizza to adding to a quiche, tart, or savory pie filling. Make a double batch. You won't be sorry.

---

3 medium-size yellow onions, halved and thinly sliced (about 5 cups)

¼ cup extra-virgin olive oil

1½ tablespoons finely chopped fresh thyme leaves

¾ teaspoon kosher salt, plus extra as needed

½ cup plus 2 tablespoons full-fat sour cream

⅓ cup mayonnaise

1½ tablespoons finely chopped fresh chives

Heaping ¼ teaspoon garlic powder

Potato chips, crackers, or carrot and celery sticks, for serving

---

1. Adjust an oven rack to the middle position and preheat the oven to 300°F.

2. Place the onions on a rimmed sheet pan and drizzle with the olive oil. Sprinkle with the thyme, stir to combine, and cover the sheet pan with aluminum foil. Bake until the onions are soft and wilted, 25 minutes. Uncover the pan, stir the onions, and continue to cook until the onions are very soft, sticky, and golden brown, 20 to 30 minutes more. Remove the sheet pan from the oven, sprinkle the onions with ½ teaspoon salt, and set aside to cool completely.

3. Whisk the sour cream, mayonnaise, chives, garlic powder, and remaining ¼ teaspoon salt in a large bowl. Stir in the cooled onions and taste, adding more salt if needed. Serve with potato chips, crackers, or carrot and celery sticks.

# OVEN-ROASTED OKRA CHIPS WITH DILL PICKLE DIP

**GF** *SERVES 4*

O kra is known to get a little slimy when cooked, thanks to the seeds in the pod. But halve the pods lengthwise and roast them and you get a crisp and wonderful chip-like veggie—no slime!—that is the perfect shape for dipping. If you have extra dill pickle dip, save it for chips, tacos (really!), or a sandwich.

---

### FOR THE DIP
½ cup full-fat sour cream
3 tablespoons buttermilk
   (see Note, page 4)
2 tablespoons very finely chopped
   dill pickles or cornichon pickles
1 tablespoon pickle juice (from a jar
   of pickles; see box)
1 teaspoon finely chopped fresh dill

¼ teaspoon kosher salt
¼ teaspoon freshly ground black
   pepper

### FOR THE OKRA
1¼ pounds okra, stem ends removed,
   pods halved lengthwise
¼ cup extra-virgin olive oil
¾ teaspoon kosher salt

---

1. Adjust an oven rack to the middle position and preheat the oven to 400°F.

2. To make the dip: In a medium-size bowl, mix together the sour cream, buttermilk, pickles, pickle juice, dill, ¼ teaspoon salt, and pepper. Cover the bowl with plastic wrap and refrigerate until serving (or for up to 5 days).

3. To roast the okra: In a large bowl, toss the okra with the olive oil and ¾ teaspoon salt. Turn the okra out onto a rimmed sheet pan and roast, stirring 2 or 3 times, until it is very crisp and browned, 20 to 25 minutes.

4. Remove from the oven and serve with the dip.

## In a Pickle

If you're pouring pickle juice down the drain after emptying the jar, you are really missing out! You can add it to anything you'd add vinegar to, like a vinaigrette or to bring an acidic component into a pan sauce. I've even been known to drizzle it into lentil soup or a salsa for that extra twang.

# SESAME-MISO KALE CHIPS

**V** **GF** *SERVES 4*

**M**y son Julian is obsessed with kale chips. I love to buy them for him but—*whoa*—they are pricey! It's infinitely more cost effective to make them myself and, thankfully, kale chips are pretty easy to make, too. Here, miso paste and soy sauce add salty richness to the kale as it slow bakes in the oven. I bake the chips on a cooling rack placed on a rimmed sheet pan. This helps the warm air circulate so the leaves don't brown on the pan but rather dry out evenly. Sometimes I'll throw kale chips into a spice grinder to make miso kale dust—sprinkled over popcorn, it's the best! Also, one half pound of kale gets gobbled up fast; making a double batch is a smart move—simply bake one sheet pan on the upper-middle oven rack and another on the lower-middle rack and swap their places midway through cooking.

---

½ pound curly kale, stems removed, leaves separated into 2 long strips, cut crosswise into thirds
3 tablespoons white miso paste (see box, page 24)

2 tablespoons soy sauce
2 tablespoons toasted sesame oil
1 teaspoon sugar
½ teaspoon kosher salt

---

**1.** Adjust an oven rack to the middle position and preheat the oven to 225°F. Place a wire rack on top of a rimmed sheet pan.

**2.** Wash the kale and spin it dry with a salad spinner. Dry each leaf with a clean kitchen towel—it's important that the leaves are very dry.

## Miso Delicious

Miso adds a naturally salty, umami (savory) flavor to sauces, dressings, soups, glazes, and spice pastes (like for these Sesame-Miso Kale Chips). White miso is the mildest tasting while red miso is the most robust. It can be fermented with a host of ingredients from soybeans to barley, rice, wheat, buckwheat, quinoa, and even hemp seeds. Miso can be found in the produce area of your supermarket or in the refrigerated aisle of health food stores near other fermented foods, such as tofu, tempeh, and the like. It keeps for months refrigerated.

3. Whisk the miso paste, soy sauce, sesame oil, sugar, and salt in a large bowl. Add the kale leaves. Toss and rub them to coat evenly with the paste, but don't massage them as you would for a kale salad—you're just coating the leaves.

4. Lay the leaves on top of the wire rack—do not overlap them—if there's not enough room on the rack, roast them in batches. Slow roast the leaves, undisturbed, until crisp, 45 to 55 minutes.

5. Remove from the oven, cool completely, and serve immediately or store in an airtight container for up to 1 day. (They don't stay crisp for long-term storage.)

# SUPER SEEDY POWER BARS

(VO) (GF) *MAKES 8 BARS*

I gave one of these bars to a friend who was running a ten-mile race and you know what? He positively glided past me at mile nine with all the energy in the world! Now, I'm not saying these bars were the source of his stamina, but I'm not saying they weren't, either. Not too sweet nor too dry, these chewy protein bars are loaded with good stuff from dates to tahini, and four kinds of seeds—including omega-3-heavy flaxseed (or hemp seed if you like—I love hemp seed for the extra protein it provides). Use sticky-soft dates such as Medjool—if the bars are made with dried-out dates, you may have a hard time shaping them.

---

1½ cups rolled oats
1 cup finely chopped soft, pitted dates (about 6 ounces)
½ cup roasted, salted sunflower seeds
⅓ cup honey or maple syrup
¼ cup finely shredded unsweetened coconut

¼ cup tahini (sesame paste; see box, page 26)
2 tablespoons sesame seeds
2 tablespoons poppy seeds
2 tablespoons flaxseed or hemp seeds
½ teaspoon kosher salt
Flaky salt, for sprinkling (optional)

---

1. Adjust an oven rack to the middle position and preheat the oven to 350°F. Line a rimmed sheet pan with parchment paper and set aside.

2. Combine the oats, dates, sunflower seeds, honey, coconut, tahini, sesame seeds, poppy seeds, flaxseed, and kosher salt in a large bowl. Knead the mixture with your hands until it is very sticky and well combined.

3. Divide the mixture into 8 heaping ¼-cup mounds. Take one mound, press it in your palms into a flattened oval shape, and place it on the prepared sheet pan. Press it to flatten and widen one side. Turn the bar on its side and press lightly to flatten the edge. Turn it over to the other wide, flat side and press down on the bar lightly to flatten it. With your hands, press and square the edges until the bars are about 4½ inches long and 2 inches wide. Set on the prepared sheet pan and repeat with the

remaining mounds. Sprinkle the tops of the bars with flaky salt (if using).

4. Bake the bars until they are browned around the edges, 16 to 18 minutes. Remove from the oven and cool completely before eating. To store, place the bars in an airtight container—they keep for a few weeks!

**NOTE:** These make a very hearty bar—for a smaller snack, halve them crosswise for 16 squares.

## Tahini: Buy It, Love It, Use It

Tahini is to sesame seeds what peanut butter is to peanuts. It's essentially sesame seeds ground with a little vegetable oil to make a paste. It's known best as one of the key ingredients in hummus and babaghanouj. It can be very pale beige-white or deep brown, and even black, the color depending on the type of sesame seed used and how heavily roasted it is. It has way more potential than just being used in Middle Eastern dishes—and I'm always thinking up new ways to put it to work—like combining it with maple syrup or honey for a glaze or syrup (see page 191), folding it into granola bars, diluting it with water for a salad dressing, or turning it into a drizzle for a grain bowl.

Try to source unhulled tahini if possible—this is made from unhulled sesame seeds and has more nutritional value than tahini made from hulled seeds—similar to choosing a whole-grain loaf of bread over white bread.

Tahini is loaded with protein, iron, calcium, potassium, and heart-healthy unsaturated fats. It keeps you fuller longer and gives you a feeling of satiety that comes with eating rich foods. . . . However, this rich food is super good for you. It's infinitely useful, very affordable, and most definitely deserves a spot in your refrigerator. Look for it in the aisle with the nut butters.

# Chapter 2

# SOUPS AND SALADS

**W**hen you grab a sheet pan, "soup" or "salad" may not be the first thing that comes to mind. Actually, my very favorite recipe in this entire book is in this chapter—Marlon's Chickpea and Winter Squash Stew with Crispy Tofu (page 35). It's delicious, it's surprisingly straightforward, and it's incredibly healthy. It's one of those dishes that just *feels good* to eat. Many recipes in this chapter fill that bill, being loaded with veggies and other good-for-you ingredients. Here, you'll find a salad confetti-sprinkled with pretty "petals" of roasted root vegetables. (Ever had roasted radishes? Prepare to have your mind blown.) There's another with golden roasted carrots so tender you can cut them with a spoon, and a summery roasted potato salad with barbecued tempeh that is a winner for picnics and other take-along outdoorsy events. Doesn't sound like the same-old soup and salad chapter, does it?

# ROASTED TOMATO GAZPACHO WITH TOASTY CROUTONS

(V) *SERVES 4*

**A** bowl of chilled gazpacho on a hot day is like a tonic. I even like eating it for breakfast—think of it as a red smoothie! Here I combine roasted tomatoes with raw cucumber, red bell pepper, and shallots, plus garlic, of course, and buzz them into a delicious gazpacho that pulls together the deep, rich intensity you get from roasting tomatoes with the freshness of the raw veggies. I like to add a few croutons before serving, but you could finish with a drizzle of kefir (a pourable savory yogurt) over the top or chopped avocado instead, if you prefer. If you like a thinner gazpacho, have a little tomato juice on hand to thin out the mixture after processing.

---

8 medium-size ripe tomatoes, cored and quartered

⅓ cup plus ¼ cup extra-virgin olive oil, plus extra for serving

1 teaspoon sweet paprika

3 teaspoons kosher salt, plus extra as needed

½ teaspoon freshly ground black pepper

3 slices (each ½ to ¾ inch thick) good-quality bread, cut into ½- to ¾-inch cubes

2 medium-size shallots, roughly chopped

2 garlic cloves, roughly chopped

1 medium-size cucumber, peeled, halved (seeds scooped out if they are large), and roughly chopped

1 medium-size red bell pepper, stemmed, seeded, and roughly chopped

3 tablespoons sherry vinegar, plus extra as needed

½ to 1 teaspoon sugar

6 large fresh basil leaves, stacked, rolled, and thinly sliced crosswise into ribbons

---

**1.** Adjust an oven rack to the middle position and preheat the oven to 375°F.

**2.** Place the tomato quarters, 2 tablespoons olive oil, the paprika, 1 teaspoon salt, and pepper in a large bowl and toss to season the tomatoes. Turn the tomatoes out onto a rimmed sheet pan, spread them into an even layer, and roast until they are very soft and deflated, 1 hour to 1 hour and 15 minutes. Increase the oven temperature to 400°F. With a rubber spatula, scrape the tomatoes and the juices from the sheet pan into the bowl of a food processor fitted with a metal blade or in a blender. Wipe the sheet pan clean.

3. Add the bread cubes to the sheet pan and season them with 2 tablespoons olive oil and 1 teaspoon salt; use your hands to toss them around a bit to evenly coat them. Toast the bread cubes until they are golden brown, 10 to 12 minutes. Remove from the oven and set the croutons aside.

4. To the tomatoes add the shallots, garlic, cucumber, red bell pepper, ⅓ cup olive oil, sherry vinegar, ½ teaspoon sugar, and 1 teaspoon salt. Process until well combined. Taste and add more sugar, salt, or vinegar if needed. Transfer to an airtight container and refrigerate for at least 2 hours. The gazpacho can be made up to 3 days ahead; it will keep longer in the refrigerator, but the garlic and onion flavors will intensify.

5. Divide the gazpacho among 4 bowls. Drizzle each with a little olive oil and add a handful of croutons. Sprinkle with basil and serve.

## Basil That Doesn't Blacken

Basil leaves are incredibly sensitive. Treat them roughly and they turn from bright green to bruised and blackened nearly instantaneously. To avoid this, use basil right after cutting it and slice it right—meaning stack the leaves, roll them into a thin cylinder, and slice them crosswise, trying to use just a single stroke. The more you rock your knife back and forth, the more bruised your basil will become.

# CUCUMBER SOUP WITH ROASTED BEETS AND POTATOES

**GF** *SERVES 4*

T his is a melding of two fantastic chilled soups: cucumber soup and borscht. Here, though, the beets become the garnish along with baby marble potatoes, dill, and chives, while the cucumber is blended with dried mint and kefir (a thin, drinkable plain yogurt) to make a lustrous soup base. Of course, you can nix the beet and potato topper and just serve the cucumber soup solo with chives and dill, but then your sheet pan would get lonely and potentially resentful. And nothing is worse than a sheet pan with a chip on its shoulder.

---

½ pound marble potatoes or very small potatoes (halved or quartered if not bite-size)

2½ tablespoons extra-virgin olive oil

2 teaspoons kosher salt, plus extra as needed

2 medium-size beets, peeled and chopped into ½-inch pieces (see box, page 96)

1 tablespoon finely chopped fresh dill

1 tablespoon finely chopped fresh chives, plus extra for garnish

3 medium-size cucumbers (¾ pound), peeled and roughly chopped

2 cups plain kefir, preferably full-fat (see Note)

½ cup sour cream, plus extra for garnish

¼ medium-size white onion, roughly chopped

1 tablespoon dried mint (optional; ideally, use the freshest dried mint you can find, see page 32)

1 tablespoon fresh lemon juice, plus extra as needed

Ice water, for thinning

---

**1.** Preheat the oven to 400°F. Line a rimmed sheet pan with aluminum foil.

**2.** Combine the potatoes, 1½ teaspoons olive oil, and ¼ teaspoon salt in a medium-size bowl and toss to coat. Turn the potatoes out onto one side of the sheet pan, spreading them into a single layer. Add the beets to the bowl with another 1½ teaspoons olive oil and another ¼ teaspoon salt. Toss to combine. Turn the beets onto the other side of the sheet pan, spreading them out as well. (You can create a border by folding a sheet of aluminum foil and wedging it between the edges of the sheet pan crosswise to create two distinct sections; this helps keep the red beets from bleeding into the other vegetables.)

3. Cover the pan with aluminum foil (you may need 2 sheets), crimping it around the edges of the pan to seal. Roast the vegetables for 20 minutes. Remove the sheet pan from the oven, uncover, and give the vegetables a stir (keeping them separate so the beets don't stain the potatoes. Remove any potatoes that are tender. Wearing oven mitts, cover the pan again and continue to roast until all the vegetables are tender, 10 to 20 minutes. Remove from the oven and place the potatoes in one bowl and the beets in another bowl. Stir the dill into the potatoes and the chives into the beets. Set aside.

4. Combine the cucumbers, kefir, sour cream, onion, mint (if using), lemon juice, and 1½ teaspoons salt in a blender; blend until smooth, adding ice water by the tablespoonful if necessary to thin to your desired consistency. Taste and add more salt if needed. (At this point the cucumber soup can be refrigerated in an airtight container for up to 1 day; for an extra-silky texture, strain the soup before refrigerating.)

5. Pour the soup into 4 bowls. Divide the warm potatoes and warm beets among the bowls, dollop with sour cream, and sprinkle with chives. Drizzle with the remaining olive oil and serve.

NOTE: No kefir? No problem. Stir together ¾ cup plain yogurt—not Greek yogurt—and ¼ cup milk until smooth.

## DIY: Microwave Dried Herbs

I took a cooking class at the Academia Barilla in Parma, Italy, where my Italian instructor had recently returned from California, where he lived for many years cooking very fresh and healthy Cal-Ital cuisine. He demonstrated an ingenious trick he has for drying herbs: Simply place the herbs in a single layer on a paper towel, cover with another paper towel, and microwave until dried. (I like doing this in 20-second increments—you don't want to overcook the herbs and remove all the flavor.) The herbs come out as if frozen in time, permanently curled like falling autumn leaves. They are still vibrant, still very green, but can be easily crushed between your fingers.

I like to force the leaves through a fine-mesh sieve for a powder that is green and positively packed with fresh herb flavor. The technique works particularly well with tender herbs such as basil, mint, parsley, tarragon, and cilantro. The dried, herbs can be stored for a few months in an airtight container—of course, the sooner you use them, the fresher and more prominent the herb flavor will be.

# CHILLED AVOCADO AND ROASTED GARLIC SOUP

GF  *SERVES 4*

Creamy, semisweet, and tangy from the kefir, this soup could easily be poured into a tall glass for a killer post-workout savory smoothie!

Roasted garlic is one of those ingredients that you might not think you'll use, but once you have a stockpile in the fridge, you'll use it *constantly*. I love having these little flavor powerhouses ready to go when I'm cooking. Roasted garlic lends sweetness and a wonderful caramelized flavor to sauces, vinaigrettes, soups, spreads . . . You name it. Roast an extra head or two and keep refrigerated. (I like to put the whole roasted head in an airtight container and refrigerate it for up to 1 week.) You can also squeeze the cloves out of the head and refrigerate them, covered with olive oil, in a very small jar for up to a few weeks, or squeeze the garlic from the head and freeze it in small quantities in a freezer-safe container to have ready to use.

---

1 head garlic
2 tablespoons extra-virgin olive oil
½ cup slivered almonds
1½ teaspoons kosher salt, plus extra as needed
2 avocados, halved, pitted, flesh scooped from the skin
1 large cucumber, peeled, halved (seeds scooped out if they are very large), and roughly chopped
1 cup plain kefir (see Note, page 32)
¼ medium-size sweet onion, such as Vidalia, roughly chopped
12 medium-size to large fresh mint leaves, roughly chopped
Juice of ½ lemon, plus extra as needed
½ cup cold water, plus extra as needed
½ cup ice cubes
½ cup crumbled ricotta salata cheese
Fresh cilantro leaves, for serving
Lemon wedges, for serving

---

1. Adjust an oven rack to the middle position and preheat the oven to 375°F.

2. With a bread knife, slice off the top third of the garlic head, exposing the inner cloves. Place the head on a piece of aluminum foil and drizzle

1 teaspoon olive oil over the top. Wrap the foil around the head and place it on a rimmed sheet pan. Place the almonds on the other side of the sheet pan and toss with 1 teaspoon olive oil and ¼ teaspoon salt. Roast until the almonds are golden brown, 7 to 8 minutes.

3. Remove the sheet pan from the oven. With a spatula, transfer the almonds to a small plate and set aside. Return the garlic to the oven and continue to roast until a paring knife inserted from the top down slips easily into a clove without resistance, 30 to 35 minutes more. Remove from the oven and set aside to cool.

4. Combine the avocados and cucumber in a blender. Squeeze 5 garlic cloves from the head and add them to the blender (save the rest for another time) along with the kefir, onion, mint, lemon juice, cold water, ice cubes, and remaining 1¼ teaspoons salt. Blend until the mixture is smooth and flecked with mint. Taste and adjust the seasoning with more salt or lemon juice if needed. Add more cold water to thin the soup if needed.

5. Divide the soup among 4 bowls. Drizzle 1 teaspoon olive oil over each serving. Sprinkle the cheese over the top, followed by the toasted almonds and cilantro, and serve with lemon wedges.

# MARLON'S CHICKPEA AND WINTER SQUASH STEW WITH CRISPY TOFU

Ⓥ ⒼⒻ *SERVES 4*

S tew on a sheet pan?? Yes! And not just any stew, but great stew. Marlon Aitcheson, a vegan chef who has cooked for celebrity rappers, actors, and artists, made this for me on the fly one night—I admit, I doubted it would turn out okay. (You know, stew on a sheet pan?) Not only did it turn out great, but it blew me away with its freshness, its variety, and its simplicity. I ate it for breakfast and dinner for several days and lamented its finish. Good thing I wrote down the recipe so I can make it again and again and again (and share it with you). This recipe is easiest if you have two sheet pans (or even one sheet pan and a baking dish for the tofu). If you don't have a second sheet pan, roast the tofu before or after the squash.

---

5 tablespoons extra-virgin olive oil
1 block (14 ounces) firm or extra-firm tofu, drained and cut into ¾-inch cubes
3 teaspoons kosher salt, plus extra as needed
1½ pounds winter squash, unpeeled, halved, seeded, and cut into ¾-inch cubes (see Note)
4 cups hot water
1 can (15½ ounces) chickpeas, drained and rinsed

6 plum tomatoes, cored and chopped into bite-size pieces
1 small yellow onion, chopped into bite-size pieces
1 small zucchini, chopped into bite-size pieces
3 garlic cloves, roughly chopped
4 large fresh sage leaves, finely chopped
¼ teaspoon crushed red pepper flakes (optional)
½ teaspoon freshly ground black pepper

---

1. Adjust an oven rack to the middle position and preheat the oven to 400°F.

2. Lightly coat a rimmed sheet pan with 1 tablespoon olive oil and add the tofu to the pan. Sprinkle the tofu

with ½ teaspoon salt, turn it and season the other side with another ½ teaspoon of salt. Roast until crisp on the bottom, 25 to 30 minutes. Transfer the tofu to a large plate and set aside.

3. Place the squash in a large bowl and toss with 1 tablespoon olive oil and 1 teaspoon salt. Arrange the squash, skin-side down, on the sheet pan. (Don't wash the bowl; you'll use it in Step 4.) Place the sheet pan in the oven and carefully pour 2 cups of the hot water into the pan so it surrounds the squash pieces. Roast the squash until tender but still holding its shape, about 30 minutes, turning the pieces over midway through cooking.

4. Meanwhile, toss together the chickpeas, tomatoes, onion, zucchini, garlic, and sage with the remaining 3 tablespoons olive oil and the remaining teaspoon of salt in the bowl you used for the squash. Add the mixture to the squash along with 2 more cups of hot water. Cover the sheet pan with aluminum foil and cook until the tomatoes are soft, the vegetables are tender, and the squash has begun to break down, about 30 minutes. Transfer the vegetable mixture and all the liquid to a large bowl.

5. Stir the vegetable mixture to break down the tomatoes. Stir in the crushed red pepper flakes (if using) and pepper. Taste and season with more salt if needed. Stir in the tofu and serve in bowls.

NOTE: I prefer kabocha, delicata, or kuri squash here because they don't have to be peeled. If using Hubbard or Calabaza squash, peel it before roasting.

# BARBECUED TEMPEH AND ROASTED POTATO SALAD

**V** **GF** *SERVES 4*

Tempeh is made from whole, fermented soybeans pressed together into a thin slab. It has a wonderfully nutty, hearty flavor and great texture—it reminds me of chewy farro or wheat berries. Here it is roasted to coax out its flavor, then doused with barbecue sauce for sweetness and spice. While the tempeh and potatoes roast, mix the celery slivers, chiles, and herbs with the vinegar, oil, salt, and pepper to half-pickle them. The result is a potato salad with lots of crunch and tenderness (plus fiber, protein, and B vitamins) that can easily be a main course or a side dish to Hoisin-Glazed Beet Loaf (page 138) or Black Bean and Quinoa Veggie Burgers (page 123). Bonus—it's super pack-along picnic friendly.

1 pound baby potatoes, scrubbed, patted dry, and halved lengthwise (I use a multi-variety bag with mini purple potatoes, Yukon Golds, and red potatoes)

2 garlic cloves, minced

1 tablespoon finely chopped fresh rosemary leaves

3 tablespoons plus 1 teaspoon extra-virgin olive oil

1¼ teaspoons kosher salt

1 large celery stalk, very thinly sliced on a diagonal

¼ cup fresh basil leaves, stacked, rolled, and thinly sliced crosswise into ribbons

3 tablespoons finely chopped fresh chives

1 small serrano or red Fresno chile, stemmed (seeded for reduced heat, if you like) and finely chopped (optional; the red Fresno packs less heat than the mighty serrano!)

1 tablespoon distilled white vinegar

1 package (8 ounces) tempeh, crumbled (see Note)

¼ teaspoon freshly ground black pepper

⅓ cup barbecue sauce

1. Adjust an oven rack to the middle position and preheat the oven to 400°F. Line a rimmed sheet pan with parchment paper or a silicone mat.

2. Toss the potato halves with the garlic, rosemary, 2 tablespoons olive oil, and ½ teaspoon salt in a medium-size bowl. Turn the potatoes out onto the prepared sheet pan, spreading them in a single layer.

3. Roast the potatoes until they are browned on the bottom, about 20 minutes. While the potatoes roast, combine the celery, basil, chives, chile (if using), vinegar, 1 teaspoon olive oil, and ¼ teaspoon salt in a large bowl and stir to combine. Set aside to let the celery pickle.

4. Place the tempeh in a small bowl and toss with the remaining 1 tablespoon olive oil, the remaining ½ teaspoon salt, and the pepper.

5. Remove the sheet pan from the oven. With a spatula, flip the potato pieces and push them to one side of the pan. Turn the tempeh out onto the other side of the pan, spreading it into an even layer. Return the sheet pan to the oven for 10 minutes.

6. Increase the oven temperature to 450°F. Pour the barbecue sauce over the tempeh (not the potatoes) turning the tempeh in the sauce with a spatula so it is evenly coated. Return the sheet pan to the oven to warm the sauce and get it sizzling, 8 to 10 minutes. Remove from the oven and set aside.

7. Add the roasted potatoes and tempeh to the celery mixture and toss to combine. The texture and flavor are best if the salad is allowed to sit at room temperature for 20 minutes before serving, but it will keep, covered and refrigerated, for up to 1 day.

NOTE: Some brands of tempeh contain gluten. If you want to make this gluten free, be sure to read the label first.

# SPICED CARROT SALAD WITH CREAMY BASIL DRESSING

(VO) (GF)  *SERVES 4*

There are few vegetables that become sexier after roasting than long, slender carrots. Their once-rigid selves swoon under the heat, becoming tender and sweet. (I like serving them long so I can eat the carrots with my fingers, but if you have better table manners than I do, cut them into thirds.) In this salad I partner the carrots with a green goddess-ish dressing made from buttery avocado and a little buttermilk (or soy or almond milk with a splash of fresh lemon juice for a dairy-free version) with lots of fresh basil. For extra flavor, I "pre-dress" the greens with a little olive oil and a splash of vinegar.

---

### FOR THE SPICED CARROTS
8 medium-size carrots, halved
   lengthwise (and cut into thirds
   crosswise, if you like)
3 tablespoons extra-virgin olive oil
1 teaspoon ground cumin
½ teaspoon sweet paprika
½ teaspoon kosher salt
¼ teaspoon ground cinnamon
¼ teaspoon ground ginger
¼ teaspoon freshly ground black
   pepper

### FOR THE DRESSING
½ avocado, peeled and pitted
¼ cup buttermilk (or soy or almond
   milk; see headnote), plus extra as
   needed

2 tablespoons extra-virgin olive oil
1 teaspoon white wine vinegar,
   plus extra as needed
1 cup fresh basil leaves
½ teaspoon kosher salt, plus extra
   as needed
¼ teaspoon freshly ground black
   pepper, plus extra as needed

### FOR THE SALAD
1 tablespoon extra-virgin olive oil
1 teaspoon white wine vinegar
¼ teaspoon kosher salt
¼ teaspoon freshly ground black
   pepper
4 cups arugula
2 cups sunflower sprouts,
   microgreens, or watercress

---

1. To roast the carrots: Adjust an oven rack to the middle position and preheat the oven to 400°F.

2. Place the carrots in a large bowl and toss with the olive oil. Mix the cumin, paprika, salt, cinnamon, ginger, and pepper in a small bowl and add to the carrots, tossing them to coat. Turn the carrots out onto a rimmed sheet pan and roast until they begin to brown, about 15 minutes. Shake the pan to move them around and continue to roast until the carrots are golden brown and tender, 10 to 15 minutes more. Remove from the oven and set aside.

3. To make the dressing: Combine the avocado, buttermilk, olive oil, vinegar, basil, salt, and pepper in a blender. Pulse until smooth and creamy. Taste and adjust with more vinegar, salt, or pepper if needed. (If the consistency is too thick, thin it with more buttermilk or water.)

4. To make the salad: Whisk the oil, vinegar, salt, and pepper in a large bowl. Add the arugula and toss gently to combine. Turn the salad out onto a platter. Arrange the carrots over the top and drizzle with the creamy basil dressing. Sprinkle with the sprouts and serve.

## Troubleshooting the Dark

Vegetables totally succumb to pure sweetness when roasted on a sheet pan, but if they get too dark (or—*gasp*—burnt!), they become bitter. If your vegetables look like they are taking on too much char before they become totally tender, reduce the oven temp or open the door for a few minutes to let some of the heat out. You can also bump the sheet pan up to a higher oven rack or buffer it by placing a second sheet pan under the already hot one (be careful not to burn yourself!)—or simply transfer the vegetables onto a clean, unheated sheet pan and finish their cooking. Another option is to remove the sheet pan from the oven for 10 minutes, then return it to the oven. This gives the pan time to cool a little so you can finish roasting the vegetables without fear of burning them. Remember—you are the master of your sheet pan (not the other way around).

# SPINACH, ROASTED ROOT "PETALS," PISTACHIOS, AND HONEY VINAIGRETTE

VO GF  *SERVES 4*

R adishes and beets. Roast them and they look almost almost like the most beautiful flower petals—so delicate, so colorful, and obviously so tasty, too. I toss the roots with spinach and pistachios for a hearty salad that can easily do you right for dinner (even better—it can be made ahead; see Step 2). The warm and gingery honey vinaigrette adds a hint of savory sweetness to the mix. Use any fresh herbs—in the singular or in combination—in this salad. I use whatever I have handy—you should do the same.

## FOR THE ROOT "PETALS"
8 ounces radishes, tops and ends trimmed, radishes halved (or quartered if large)

3 medium-size carrots, tops and ends trimmed, carrots halved lengthwise and sliced crosswise into thirds on a diagonal

1 pound small beets, tops and ends trimmed, beets halved lengthwise, and thinly sliced lengthwise into long half-moons (I like a combination of red and yellow beets)

¼ cup extra-virgin olive oil

1 teaspoon kosher salt

1 medium-size red onion, halved and thinly sliced

## FOR THE SALAD
⅓ cup extra-virgin olive oil

2 teaspoons grated fresh ginger

½ teaspoon ground coriander

1 tablespoon honey or agave syrup

3 tablespoons sherry vinegar

¼ teaspoon kosher salt

¼ teaspoon freshly ground black pepper

6 cups fresh baby spinach or roughly chopped large spinach leaves

¼ cup roughly chopped fresh herbs (such as basil, cilantro, dill, mint, fennel fronds, parsley, marjoram, or tarragon)

½ cup toasted, salted shelled pistachios

1. To roast the root "petals": Adjust an oven rack to the middle position and preheat the oven to 375°F.

2. Toss the radishes, carrots, and yellow beets, if using, with 2 tablespoons olive oil and ½ teaspoon salt. Turn them out onto a rimmed sheet pan and push them to one side. Add the red beets and red onion to the bowl and toss with the remaining olive oil and salt. Place them on the other side of the pan. (You can create a border by folding a sheet of aluminum foil and wedging it between the edges of the sheet pan crosswise to create two distinct sections; this helps keep the red beets from bleeding into the other vegetables.) Roast until browned on the bottom, about 20 minutes. Shake the pan, and flip the vegetables with a spatula, taking care to keep the red beets separated from the other vegetables. Continue to roast until tender, about 10 minutes more. Remove from the oven and set aside. (The roasted roots will keep at room temperature for up to 6 hours, or in an airtight container in the refrigerator for up to 3 days. Reheat them in a warm oven until they lose their chill, 10 minutes, before proceeding.)

3. To make the salad: Place the olive oil in a small pan with the ginger and coriander and cook over medium heat until the ginger is fragrant, 30 seconds to 1 minute. Stir in the honey and cook for 20 seconds more. Turn off the heat and pour the honey mixture into a large bowl. Whisk in the sherry vinegar, salt, and pepper until the dressing is creamy, about 10 seconds. Pour half the vinaigrette into a small bowl and set aside. To the remaining vinaigrette in the bowl add the spinach and herbs and toss to combine.

4. Arrange the dressed greens on a platter and scatter the roasted vegetables over the top. Drizzle with the reserved vinaigrette, sprinkle with pistachios, and serve.

# SWEET POTATO, BLUE CHEESE, AND PECAN SALAD

**VO** **GF** *SERVES 4*

On a holiday brunch or dinner table, no salad can beat this one—sweet potatoes roasted until golden and tender, paired with toasted pecans, blue cheese, and a sherry vinaigrette. You could add leafy greens—you *could*—but the mere absence of salad greens somehow makes the dish more decadent and delicious (the finely chopped arugula really serves more as an herb than as a leafy green here). Pecan halves make for a prettier presentation but pieces can be more economical—either way you go, know it will taste equally delicious.

---

2 sweet potatoes, chopped into ½-inch pieces (I like to leave the skin on)

5 tablespoons extra-virgin olive oil

1½ teaspoons plus a pinch of kosher salt, plus extra as needed

¼ teaspoon crushed red pepper flakes

¾ cup raw pecan halves or pieces

1 tablespoon maple syrup

½ small shallot, finely chopped

2 tablespoons sherry vinegar

1 teaspoon Dijon mustard

¼ teaspoon freshly ground black pepper, plus extra as needed

½ cup arugula leaves, very finely chopped

½ cup crumbled blue cheese (optional)

---

**1.** Adjust an oven rack to the middle position and preheat the oven to 375°F.

**2.** Place the sweet potatoes in a medium-size bowl and toss them with 2 tablespoons olive oil, 1 teaspoon salt, and the crushed red pepper flakes. Turn the sweet potatoes out onto a rimmed sheet pan and spread into an even layer (save the bowl for the pecans in Step 3). Roast until they start to brown, about 15 minutes.

**3.** While the sweet potatoes roast, toss the pecans with 1 tablespoon olive oil, the maple syrup, and ½ teaspoon salt in the bowl used for the sweet potatoes. Pull the sweet potatoes out of the oven and, with a spatula, flip them and scooch them to one side of the pan. Turn the pecans out onto the other side of the pan. Return the sheet pan to the oven and roast until the sweet potatoes are tender and the pecans are fragrant and toasted, 8 to 10 minutes more. Remove from the oven and set aside (the sweet potatoes will keep at room temperature for up to 6 hours, or in an airtight container in the refrigerator for up to 3 days).

4. When ready to serve, whisk the shallot, vinegar, mustard, a pinch of salt, and the pepper in a small bowl. Whisk in the remaining 2 tablespoons olive oil, taste, and adjust the salt or pepper if needed. (The dressing should taste slightly acidic to balance the potatoes that are already dressed with oil.) Pour the dressing over the sweet potatoes and pecans. Add the arugula, toss to combine, sprinkle with blue cheese, and serve.

# MOROCCAN COUSCOUS SALAD WITH OLIVES, CHICKPEAS, AND ROASTED TOMATOES

**(vo)** *SERVES 4*

Couscous is a great base for any number of roasted vegetables and beans, and it cooks just as easily in the oven as it does on the stovetop. Here it hangs out with some roasted tomatoes, olives, feta, and mint. This is one of my favorite quick suppers that serves double duty as a picnic/potluck salad—it just gets better and better the longer the ingredients mingle together.

Ras el hanout is a Moroccan spice blend that means "top of the spice," referring to the towering pyramids of spices available to purchase by the gram in souks across the country. The flavor is a little sweet and a little spicy, like a subdued curry powder—and like curry powder or garam masala (another wonderful Indian spice blend that's earthier and more cinnamon-y than curry), it can be made from a wildly vast array of herbs and spices from cumin to coriander, chili powder to ginger and clove. You can find it in Middle Eastern markets and even some grocery store spice aisles and, of course, online.

---

2 medium-size tomatoes, cored and finely chopped

2 tablespoons extra-virgin olive oil

1 teaspoon ras el hanout or garam masala

½ teaspoon kosher salt, plus extra as needed

½ teaspoon freshly ground black pepper, plus extra as needed

1½ cups couscous

1 can (15 ounces) chickpeas, drained and rinsed

1¼ cups boiling water

1 cup hot vegetable broth (or 1 extra cup boiling water)

Zest and juice of 1 lemon

3 scallions, finely chopped

½ cup pitted green olives (such as Castelvetrano or Picholine), finely chopped

4 ounces feta cheese, crumbled

¼ cup finely chopped fresh mint leaves

---

## Getting the Most from Winter Tomatoes

In the summertime I am an absolute tomato fiend—I can't get enough of juicy-sweet heirlooms and field tomatoes picked fresh and never refrigerated. In the cooler months when I can't get those jewels, I don't avoid tomatoes entirely—I'll buy the best-looking supermarket tomatoes and roast them to coax out some sweetness. This recipe offers a basic method for roasting tomatoes (you can skip the ras el hanout for a milder flavor). Use them right away or roast a few sheet pans full of them and freeze, in resealable freezer-safe bags, for up to 1 year.

1. Adjust an oven rack to the middle position and preheat the oven to 400°F.

2. Toss the tomatoes with 1 tablespoon olive oil, the ras el hanout, salt, and pepper in a medium-size bowl to coat. Turn them out onto a rimmed sheet pan, spreading them into an even layer. Roast until they start to soften and become juicy, 12 to 15 minutes.

3. Reduce the oven temperature to 350°F. Wearing oven mitts, carefully pull out the sheet pan partway (so it's still resting on the oven rack), add the couscous, chickpeas, boiling water, and vegetable broth to the tomatoes, and stir to incorporate. Cover the sheet pan with aluminum foil (you may need 2 sheets), crimping it tightly around the edges to seal.

4. Bake until the couscous has absorbed all the liquid, about 12 minutes. (Carefully turn up one corner of the foil and peek in to check.) Remove the sheet pan from the oven and let the couscous cool, covered, for 5 minutes.

5. Turn the couscous out into a large bowl and fluff it with a fork (or keep it on the sheet pan if you prefer). Add the lemon zest and juice, scallions, olives, feta, and remaining tablespoon olive oil and fluff again. Taste, and adjust the seasoning with more salt and pepper if needed, which will depend on how salty your feta and olives are. Stir in most of the mint; sprinkle the rest over the top. Serve warm or at room temperature, or refrigerate in an airtight container for up to 3 days and serve cold.

# ROASTED PLUM SALAD WITH FRESH GRAPEFRUIT AND CARDAMOM SYRUP

Ⓥ ⒼⒻ  *SERVES 4*

**W**hen I bring a fruit salad to a brunch or party, I always, *always* get requests for the recipe. My secret is to (a) combine roasted fruit with fresh fruit for fun textural variety (here: fresh grapefruit and roasted plums); (b) think about color and what will pop and be beautiful together (the redness of the plums with their black skin against the pink grapefruit); (c) not use too many fruits (otherwise there will be flavor confusion; that's why there are only two fruits in this fruit salad! Though note that other fruits like apricots, nectarines, mangoes, and pineapple are all great, too, and can be used in place of the plums or the grapefruit), and (d) toss the fruit with a spiced simple syrup to give it an unexpected edge (like cardamom syrup . . . yum!). Simple syrup is essentially a mixture of one part water to one part sugar that's brought to a simmer to dissolve the sugar. That's it—so easy. (You can add all kinds of spices and accents to simple syrup—see the Note on page 52 for ideas.)

The cardamom syrup in this salad lends a floral, almost Turkish, feel— a splash of rose water or orange blossom water here would not be far-fetched. The recipe makes more than you'll need for the salad, but good news: The rest can be refrigerated in an airtight container for a month. Use it to sweeten lemonade, iced coffee or tea, or hot chai; make a cocktail; drizzle over French toast or waffles. . . . You get the picture.

---

2 teaspoons neutral vegetable oil (such as grapeseed or safflower)
¼ cup plus 2 teaspoons sugar
Pinch of flaky sea salt or kosher salt
6 plums (preferably with bright red flesh), halved, pitted, and each half cut into thirds

½ teaspoon ground cardamom
Squeeze of fresh lime juice
1 Ruby Red grapefruit
1 tablespoon finely chopped fresh mint leaves, plus a few leaves for serving

---

1. Adjust an oven rack to the middle position and preheat the oven to 375°F. Line a rimmed sheet pan with parchment paper.

## Sophisticated Simples

Simple syrups are excellent for drizzling on roasted fruits, whisking with confectioners' sugar to glaze a cake, mixing into iced tea or lemonade, or using to sweeten a vinaigrette. In addition to the cardamom used in the roasted plum salad, you can season a simple syrup with a host of ingredients. Here are some of my favorites, which you can, of course, mix and match—cinnamon stick with dried red chile and ginger; vanilla with chamomile tea and lemon; or blueberries with aniseed and tarragon . . . Let your imagination run free.

- Chiles (dried red chiles, fresh jalapeños and serranos, smoked and dried chiles)

- Citrus juice, zest, slices (grapefruit, lemon, lime, orange, tangerine)

- Coffee or tea

- Fresh fruit (berries, mango, pineapple)

- Fresh ginger slices

- Sprigs of fresh herbs (basil, lavender, rosemary, sage, tarragon, thyme)

- Spices, used alone or in combination (aniseed, caraway seeds, cinnamon sticks, coriander seeds, fennel seeds, nutmeg, star anise, whole cloves)

- Vanilla beans (seeds and pod)

NOTE: Simple syrup should be refrigerated in an airtight container; it will keep for up to 1 month. You can strain out the flavor addition before using, if you like (especially any fresh ingredients if you plan to store the syrup for more than a day or two). Or you can eat the flavorings: Candied chiles, citrus zest, and fresh ginger are all delicious!

2. Whisk the vegetable oil with 2 teaspoons sugar and the salt in a large bowl. Add the plums and toss to coat. Turn the plums out onto the prepared sheet pan, flesh-side down, and roast until they are soft and slightly singed, about 20 minutes. Remove from the oven and set aside. (For an even more caramelized flavor and appearance, after roasting place the sheet pan on the top oven rack under the broiler for a few minutes to char the plums slightly around the edges.)

3. Combine ¼ cup sugar and the cardamom with ¼ cup water in a small saucepan. Bring to a simmer over medium-high heat, stirring until the sugar is dissolved, about 3 minutes. Turn off the heat and set aside to cool to room temperature. Add a squeeze of lime juice to the syrup.

4. Place the grapefruit on a cutting board and, with a sharp knife, slice off the ends to expose the segments. Slice off the rind from top to bottom, following the curve of the grapefruit to remove as little flesh as possible. With the knife, cut between the membranes to release the segments—do this over a bowl to catch the grapefruit juices.

5. Place the grapefruit segments in a serving bowl. Add the plums and reserved grapefruit juice, drizzle with 2 tablespoons cardamom syrup, and gently toss to combine. Sprinkle with the mint and serve with a few mint leaves scattered on top.

# A GOOD CHEESE SALAD WITH ROASTED PEARS AND CANDIED WALNUTS

*SERVES 4*

There is a magical moment that happens when you're in a certain kind of restaurant and dinner has ended and you feel full and happy, and like you couldn't possibly eat another bite—until that chariot of cheese arrives, the glass dome lifted by a graceful hand, the scents of age and funk and buttery goodness hitting you upside the head. This salad was inspired by that beautiful moment. The sugared walnuts add a savory-sweet note because they are candied with honey, rosemary, and black pepper—a perfect foil for the unctuousness of a great cheese. Roasted pears make the trio a balanced one. (Roast extra for breakfast to pile on your yogurt—you won't regret it.)

## FOR THE CANDIED WALNUTS

¾ cup shelled walnut halves

1½ teaspoons walnut oil or grapeseed oil

1 tablespoon honey

1 tablespoon confectioners' sugar

1 teaspoon finely chopped fresh rosemary leaves

¾ teaspoon kosher salt

½ teaspoon freshly ground black pepper

## FOR THE SALAD

2 tablespoons balsamic vinegar

2 tablespoons honey

2 ripe Bosc pears, halved and cored

2 tablespoons red wine vinegar

¼ teaspoon whole-grain mustard (optional)

Large pinch of flaky salt

Few twists of freshly ground black pepper

3 tablespoons walnut oil or grapeseed oil

4 cups salad greens (I like to combine tender ones like butter leaf with bitter ones like arugula or mizuna)

A little watercress (optional)

8 ounces perfectly ripe cheese, cut into 4 equal pieces (see box, page 54)

## Picking Perfect Cheese

I encourage you to have an open mind and choose a cheese that your cheesemonger advises you to buy right this minute (as in now) because it is oozy and ready for prime time—be it blue, goat, sheep, cow, triple cream, ashed, dunked in grappa, or so perfectly at peak runny-ripeness that you have to lob off the top and spoon it out. Sometimes it's just a beautifully aged cheese—like a clothbound farmhouse Cheddar or a very special cave-aged cheese made by monks on a mountaintop. If your market doesn't have a cheese specialist, just buy your favorite darn cheese and make it the star of the show.

1. To make the candied walnuts: Adjust an oven rack to the middle position and preheat the oven to 375°F. Line a rimmed sheet pan with parchment paper or a silicone baking mat.

2. Combine the walnuts, walnut oil, honey, confectioners' sugar, rosemary, salt, and pepper in a large bowl and toss to coat. Turn the nuts out onto the prepared sheet pan, spreading them in an even layer, and roast until fragrant and toasty, 10 to 12 minutes. Remove from the oven, lift the parchment or silicone baking mat by the corners, and transfer the nuts to a plate. Set aside to cool. Increase the oven temperature to 400°F.

3. To make the salad: Line the sheet pan with a new sheet of parchment paper (or a silicone baking mat). Whisk the balsamic vinegar and honey in a medium-size bowl. Dip each pear half, cut side down, into the balsamic honey and place the pears, cut side down, on the prepared sheet pan. Roast until the pears are tender and caramelized on the bottom, 20 to 25 minutes. Remove from the oven and set aside.

4. Whisk the red wine vinegar, mustard, salt, and pepper in a large bowl. Whisk in the walnut oil until the mixture is creamy and thick, about 10 seconds. Add the salad greens and watercress (if using), and toss to coat.

5. Divide the dressed greens among 4 plates. Add a wedge (or crumble or scoop) of the cheese on the side of each, and prop a pear half against the cheese and greens. Sprinkle the salad with the walnuts and serve.

Chapter 3

# VEGGIES WITH A SIDE OF VEGETABLES

Of course, all of the recipes in this cookbook have lots of vegetables. I mean, it is *Sheet Pan Suppers Meatless* after all—what a sad lot we'd be without our rainbow of fruits and vegetables to accompany grains and beans, breads and pasta! Of course, they can be your main course, but they can also be a happy side dish to a rice bowl or pizza—and, *yes*, I see no problem *at all* with serving tacos *and* pizza for dinner. Late summer dishes like Summer Tomato Slab Pie with Flaky Sage Crust (page 83) and spiralized Zucchini Ribbons Aglio e Olio (page 86) are both fantastic ways to use up treasures from the garden or greenmarket; the Spicy Thai Green Curry Potpie (page 69) and Hoisin Eggplant, Spicy Brussels Sprouts, and Tofu (page 59) will happily out-delicious any takeout option, and the saucy Tofu Puttanesca with Garlic Bread (page 81) and Three-Cheese Crispy Mushroom-Parm Sandwich (page 75) are just the comfort I crave on a cold night.

# BLISSED-OUT CRISPY CHEESY BROCCOLI GRATIN

*SERVES 4*

L imited surface area. This is the problem with a broccoli gratin made in a casserole-style baking dish, meaning the ratio of crispy-cheesy-crumb-y topping to soft, tender broccoli is just way under optimal balance. With a sheet pan, however, every single morsel of broccoli gets an ample coating of crunch. You know what else is awesome? With a preheated sheet pan (see box, before you get started), the time it takes to roast the broccoli is minimal—I'm talking 15 minutes, tops, for caramelized edges and florets. Meaning you can hit broccoli bliss in under 20 minutes. Are you in?

---

1¼ pounds broccoli florets
   (I like leaving about 1 inch of
   the stem attached)
2 tablespoons extra-virgin olive oil
1 teaspoon kosher salt
2 tablespoons unsalted butter
2 garlic cloves, minced

⅓ cup panko bread crumbs
¾ cup grated Cheddar cheese
¼ cup finely grated Parmigiano
   Reggiano cheese

---

1. Adjust one oven rack to the upper-middle position and another rack to the position. Place a rimmed sheet pan on the middle rack and preheat the oven to 400°F.

2. Toss the broccoli florets with the olive oil and salt in a medium-size bowl. Turn the broccoli out onto the hot sheet pan (it should sizzle!) and roast until the bottom of the florets are nicely browned, about 15 minutes.

## Preheat the Sheet

Hey, everybody! Need to roast some veggies for dinner? Preheat the sheet pan *with* the oven. This is such an A+ tip because in the same time it takes to preheat the oven you can get the sheet pan sizzling hot—meaning when you turn out those oil-tossed, salt-seasoned vegetables onto it, they get a good sear right at the top of the cooking process, similar to adding vegetables to a hot skillet. Not only does this jump-start the cooking process and decrease the total roasting time, but it also assures you'll get caramelized crispy edges and even charred bits, if that's your thing. (It's totally my thing.)

3. Meanwhile, combine the butter and garlic in a ramekin and place it in the oven until the butter melts, 5 minutes. (Alternatively, combine them in a microwave-safe bowl and microwave on high power in 15-second increments, swirling between each, until the butter melts, 45 seconds to 1 minute.)

4. Place the bread crumbs in a medium-size bowl, add the butter-garlic mixture, and toss with a fork. Add the Cheddar and Parmigiano Reggiano cheeses and toss to combine.

5. Remove the sheet pan from the oven and sprinkle the broccoli with the cheesy bread crumb mixture. Turn the broiler to high and place the sheet pan on the upper rack. Broil until the cheese is melted and browned, 1 to 2 minutes (watch the bread crumbs closely as broiler intensities vary and you don't want them to burn). Remove from the oven, transfer to a platter—making sure to scrape up all of the crispy, crunchy cheesy bits—and serve.

**So good with . . .**

Tofu Puttanesca with Garlic Bread (page 81); Crispy Roasted Shallot and Lentil Mujadara (page 133); Herby Singed-Tomato Tabouli (page 107)

# HOISIN EGGPLANT, SPICY BRUSSELS SPROUTS, AND TOFU

(V) (GF) SERVES 4

**S**riracha is nearly more popular than salsa (though perhaps by the time you read this, it will, officially, be more popular), and Korean gochujang could possibly be the next Sriracha—it tastes like a love child of miso and Sriracha, but is used more like an ingredient in a sauce or marinade rather than as a condiment. It's made from red chiles, rice, fermented soybeans, and salt and gives the Brussels sprouts and tofu in this dish a deeply burnished, slightly spicy chile taste. After you offset the Korean gochujang against the sweet, gingery hoisin eggplant, you may find yourself turning to this dinner way more than takeout!

---

1 pound Brussels sprouts, ends trimmed, sprouts halved lengthwise

¼ cup neutral vegetable oil (such as grapeseed or safflower)

1 teaspoon kosher salt

8 ounces extra-firm tofu, drained and blotted dry

2 tablespoons Korean gochujang sauce (see headnote)

2 tablespoons toasted sesame oil

2 garlic cloves, grated on a Microplane-style rasp, or minced

1½ tablespoons balsamic vinegar

1 tablespoon soy sauce

1 pound (about 3 medium-size or 2 large) Chinese or Japanese eggplant, tops removed, eggplants sliced into 1-inch pieces on a diagonal

2 tablespoons hoisin sauce

1 tablespoon grated fresh ginger

1 tablespoon mirin (rice wine)

4 scallions, thinly sliced on a diagonal

1 tablespoon toasted sesame seeds

## Does Eggplant Need to be Salted?

Are you ready to have your mind blown? You can stop salting your eggplant (and you're welcome). Salting eggplant *does not* reduce bitterness—seeds cause bitterness and if you want less bitter eggplant, just buy smaller eggplants with fewer seeds (same logic as when picking out cucumbers or zucchini—smaller is sweeter and less seedy). What salting *is* great for is for collapsing the cells inside the eggplant and releasing the water trapped in the eggplant's flesh. After releasing the water, eggplant cooks up crispier and with less sputtering and splattering, especially when panfrying.

1. Adjust an oven rack to the middle position and preheat the oven to 400°F.

2. Toss the Brussels sprouts with 2 tablespoons vegetable oil and ¾ teaspoon salt in a medium-size bowl. Place them on a rimmed sheet pan and roast until they are starting to brown, about 15 minutes.

3. Slice the tofu into ½- to ¾-inch planks. Stack the planks and cut them into 1-inch-long rectangles. Place the tofu in a large bowl, add 1 tablespoon vegetable oil, and toss to coat.

4. Push the sprouts to one side of the sheet pan and add the tofu to the other side. Roast until the bottom of the tofu is browned, about 15 minutes, then flip each piece with a spatula. Cook until the other side is golden, about 10 minutes more.

5. Whisk the gochujang, 1 tablespoon sesame oil, garlic, balsamic vinegar, and soy sauce in a medium-size bowl. Remove the sheet pan from the oven and, with a silicone basting brush, dab the sauce over the sprouts and tofu. Return the pan to the oven and cook until the sauce begins to caramelize, about 5 minutes. Transfer to a platter.

6. Place the eggplant in a large bowl and toss with the remaining tablespoon vegetable oil and ¼ teaspoon salt. Place the eggplant on a clean, rimmed sheet pan and roast until it starts to brown and soften, 10 to 12 minutes.

7. Meanwhile, whisk the hoisin, remaining tablespoon sesame oil, ginger, and mirin in a medium-size heatproof bowl. Transfer the eggplant to the bowl, toss to coat, then return the dressed eggplant to the pan and continue to roast until it is tender, about 5 minutes more. With a spatula, place the eggplant over the sprouts and tofu. Sprinkle with the scallions and sesame seeds and serve.

## How to Peel and Grate Ginger

Fresh ginger has a very thin, papery layer of skin that is super easy to remove—just use the side of a teaspoon to scrape it away. A vegetable peeler works fine but, in addition to removing the thin skin, you also lose some of the root—and that's like throwing money away.

The best tool I have found to grate ginger is a Microplane-style rasp—I also use this tool for grating nutmeg, citrus, garlic, and chocolate. (I have one dedicated for garlic and one for everything else, FYI.) You can also use a triangular porcelain or ceramic ginger grater; these have small sharp spikes on the surface that grate the ginger and a little trough at the bottom to collect it. They're available in Asian markets and cooking shops.

> *So good with . . .*
> Green Rice with Charred Broccoli (page 113), Hoisin-Glazed Beet Loaf (page 138)

# CARROTS WITH GARAM MASALA, CAULIFLOWER "COUSCOUS," AND PEANUT VINAIGRETTE

(V) (GF) *SERVES 4*

Saying that everyone in India uses curry powder is like saying everyone in Italy tosses their pasta with marinara. Go to India and you're more likely to see spices with names like *bottle masala* and *vadouvan* in kitchen cupboards. In the north, earthy spices such as cumin, cinnamon, cloves, and nutmeg are common and make up the flavor directive for the garam masala spice blend. These warm, sweet notes are especially complementary to carrots roasted with maple syrup and rosemary. Peanuts add protein and crunch and, served over a bed of pulverized raw cauliflower "couscous" (see box, page 64), this is a pure plant-based and gluten-free meal that satisfies on multiple levels.

---

1 pound medium-size carrots, peeled and sliced crosswise on a diagonal, ½ inch thick
¼ cup extra-virgin olive oil
1¼ teaspoons garam masala
1¼ teaspoons kosher salt
1 small head cauliflower, leaves and core removed, roughly chopped

1 tablespoon maple syrup
Juice of 1 lemon
1½ teaspoons finely chopped fresh rosemary leaves
½ cup roasted, salted peanuts, roughly chopped
2 tablespoons chopped fresh cilantro, for serving

---

1. Adjust an oven rack to the middle position, place a rimmed sheet pan on top, and preheat the oven to 425°F.

2. Toss the carrots with 2 tablespoons olive oil, the garam masala, and ½ teaspoon salt in a medium-size bowl.

3. Turn the carrots out onto the hot pan. (Don't wash the bowl—use it to make the vinaigrette in Step 5.) Wearing oven mitts, shake the pan to spread the carrots into an even layer. Roast until they are browned on one side, 10 to 12 minutes.

4. Meanwhile, place the cauliflower in a food processor and pulse until it is crumbly and looks like couscous, about eight (1-second) pulses. Add 1 tablespoon olive oil and ½ teaspoon salt. Pulse once or twice just to combine.

5. To the bowl used for the carrots, add the maple syrup, lemon juice, rosemary, remaining tablespoon olive oil, and remaining ¼ teaspoon salt. Whisk until emulsified and well combined. Add the peanuts and give it a quick stir.

6. Remove the sheet pan from the oven and pour the peanut mixture over the carrots. Use a spatula to turn the carrots in the vinaigrette. Return the pan to the oven and cook until the peanuts start to brown and the honey begins to smell caramelized, 5 to 7 minutes. Divide the cauliflower couscous among 4 plates. Divide the carrots and peanuts over the cauliflower and serve sprinkled with cilantro, warm or at room temperature.

## Make Cauli Confetti

When you blitz cauliflower in the food processor, it breaks down into baby cauliflower confetti that looks just like couscous. It makes an excellent gluten- and carbohydrate-free stand-in for wheat-based couscous. You can serve it raw (so nice and easy in the summertime), sauté it for a couple of minutes with olive oil or butter, or steam it in the microwave for 1 to 2 minutes. Sprinkle with salt and herbs and you have an unexpected alternative to wheat-based sides.

# INDIAN CREAMED SPINACH OVER POTATOES WITH TOFU

(V) (GF)  *SERVES 4*

A bright and vibrant saag sauce (essentially an Indian spinach sauce blended with loads of spices and coconut milk) is luscious ladled over crispy-roasted potatoes and tofu. The sauce stays bright green because the spinach is just barely wilted in the spiced coconut milk before blending. This tastes brilliant over cooked rice, cauliflower "couscous" (page 63), or quinoa (see page 114 for a cooking chart of basic grains and quinoa). Or, if you don't mind carb on carb (you know I don't!), with purchased naan bread wrapped in foil and warmed in the still-hot oven for a minute. If you prefer, leave out the potatoes and roast mushroom quarters, eggplant, and Brussels sprouts, or just add a can of chickpeas instead.

---

### FOR THE POTATOES AND TOFU

2 medium-size Yukon Gold potatoes, cut into ¾-inch pieces

3 tablespoons extra-virgin olive oil

¾ teaspoon kosher salt

1 block (14 ounces) firm tofu, drained and cut into ¾-inch pieces

### FOR THE INDIAN-SPICED SPINACH

1½ cups coconut milk (full fat or lite)

1½ teaspoons ground cumin

1½ teaspoons ground coriander

½ teaspoon freshly ground black pepper

¼ teaspoon ground cardamom

¼ teaspoon cayenne pepper

¼ teaspoon kosher salt

⅛ teaspoon ground cloves

1 teaspoon neutral vegetable oil (such as grapeseed or safflower)

3 garlic cloves, roughly chopped

1-inch piece fresh ginger, peeled and roughly chopped

8 ounces fresh spinach, roughly chopped (about 8 cups)

---

1. Adjust an oven rack to the middle position and preheat the oven to 450°F.

2. Place the potatoes, 2 tablespoons olive oil, and ½ teaspoon salt in a medium-size bowl and toss to combine. Turn the potatoes out onto a rimmed sheet pan (save the bowl for the tofu in Step 3) and roast, undisturbed, until browned on the bottom, about 15 minutes.

Veggies with a Side of Vegetables • **65**

3. Meanwhile, add the tofu to the bowl used for the potatoes along with the remaining tablespoon olive oil and ¼ teaspoon salt. Toss to combine.

4. With a spatula, flip the potatoes, push them to one side of the sheet pan, and add the tofu to the other side. Roast until the potatoes are tender and the tofu is crisp on the bottom, about 7 minutes. Transfer the potatoes and tofu to a large serving bowl.

5. Stir together the coconut milk, cumin, coriander, black pepper, cardamom, cayenne, salt, and cloves in a large measuring cup. Add the vegetable oil, garlic, and ginger to the sheet pan, spread it out slightly, and heat in the oven until fragrant, 30 seconds to 1 minute. Wearing oven mitts, pull out the sheet pan partway (so it's still resting on the oven rack), carefully pour the coconut milk mixture into the pan, give it a stir, and return it to the oven until it gets very hot, about 5 minutes more.

6. Place the spinach in a blender (or a large bowl if using an immersion blender) and pour the hot coconut milk mixture over the spinach. (It will wilt just enough to lose its raw taste.) Blend until completely smooth. Pour the spinach mixture over the potatoes and tofu and serve.

> ### So good with . . .
> Indian Lentils (Daal; page 135); Green Rice with Charred Broccoli (page 113); Spinach, Roasted Root "Petals," Pistachios, and Honey Vinaigrette (page 43)

# "BRAISED" CABBAGE WITH SHERRY VINAIGRETTE

(V) (GF)  *SERVES 4*

Hearty, rich, sweet, and tangy—I just love how the ruffled layers of cabbage wilt and caramelize when roasted on a sheet pan. Pouring a little acidic vinaigrette over the cabbage at the end and continuing to bake it allows the sauce to seep into the layers and some of the sharpness of the vinegar to mellow in the oven. I could totally imagine this with some veggie sausages on the side and, perhaps, a few pieces of dark pumpernickel bread.

¼ cup plus 2 tablespoons extra-virgin olive oil
1 large head green cabbage, quartered and cored
2 teaspoons kosher salt

2½ tablespoons sherry vinegar
2 teaspoons seedy Dijon mustard
1¼ teaspoons sugar
½ teaspoon freshly ground black pepper

1. Adjust an oven rack to the middle position, place a rimmed sheet pan on top, and preheat the oven to 450°F.

2. Remove the hot pan from the oven and add 2 tablespoons olive oil, tilting the pan to disperse it around the middle—the oil doesn't need to go to the edges or corners of the pan. Place the cabbage wedges, flat-side down, on the pan and drizzle 2 more tablespoons olive oil over them.

Sprinkle the cabbage wedges with 1½ teaspoons salt and roast until the bottoms start to brown, about 10 minutes.

3. Reduce the oven temperature to 325°F and, wearing oven mitts, cover the pan with aluminum foil (you may need 2 sheets), crimping it around the edges to seal. Continue to roast until the cabbage is tender to the core when pierced with a paring knife, about 15 minutes.

4. While the cabbage cooks, make the vinaigrette: Whisk the remaining 2 tablespoons olive oil, vinegar, mustard, sugar, remaining ½ teaspoon salt, and the pepper in a small bowl. Pull out the sheet pan partway (so it's still resting on the oven rack), carefully remove the foil from the sheet pan, and drizzle the vinaigrette over each wedge. Replace the foil and continue to bake the cabbage to let the vinaigrette seep into the layers, 5 minutes more.

5. Remove the pan from the oven, discard the foil, and serve.

*So good with* . . .

A Good Cheese Salad with Roasted Pears and Candied Walnuts (page 53); Creamy Carrot Polenta with Winter Squash Ragù (page 110); Slab Quiche with Spinach, Goat Cheese, and Caramelized Onions (page 186), and a simple green salad

# SPICY THAI GREEN CURRY POTPIE

*SERVES 6*

**I**n Thailand, green curry is made from lots of fresh herbs and fresh green chiles—it has nothing to do with the yellow-orange curry powder of India and the subcontinent. Green curry tastes wonderfully bright and vivacious in this potpie, especially up against the richness of coconut milk and the buttery puff pastry top crust. You can use just about any vegetable in this curry, so if you're not down with eggplant and mushrooms, try any of the following (alone or in combination, cut into bite-size pieces) as a substitute for either or both: broccoli, carrots, cauliflower, green beans, red bell peppers, small potatoes, and even Brussels sprouts.

---

1 tablespoon coriander seeds

2 teaspoons cumin seeds

1 pound eggplant, stem end removed, flesh cut into ¾-inch cubes

8 ounces mushrooms (preferably brown mushrooms or shiitakes), stemmed and caps halved or quartered if large

1 small red onion, cut into bite-size pieces

¼ cup neutral vegetable oil (such as grapeseed or safflower)

1¾ teaspoons kosher salt

1 lemongrass stalk, ends trimmed and tough outer layer(s) removed, tender reed halved lengthwise and then cut crosswise into 1-inch pieces

1 tablespoon finely chopped fresh ginger

Zest of 1 lime

5 serrano or 4 jalapeño chiles, stemmed (seeded for reduced heat, if you like) and roughly chopped

5 Thai bird's-eye chiles (or 3 extra serranos or jalapeños), stemmed (seeded for reduced heat, if you like) and roughly chopped

5 garlic cloves, roughly chopped

5 scallions, roughly chopped

⅓ cup fresh cilantro leaves with tender stems

1 can (14 to 15 ounces) lite coconut milk

2 sheets frozen puff pastry, defrosted

3 tablespoons unsalted butter, melted

1. Adjust an oven rack to the middle position and preheat the oven to 375°F.

2. Toast the seeds for the curry: Place the coriander and cumin on a doubled piece of aluminum foil with the edges slightly turned up (so the seeds don't spill over). Place the seeds in the oven and cook until fragrant and golden, 5 to 7 minutes. Transfer the seeds to a small plate and set aside.

3. Roast the vegetables for the potpie: Place the eggplant, mushrooms, and red onion in a large bowl and toss with 2 tablespoons vegetable oil and 1 teaspoon salt. Turn the eggplant mixture out onto a rimmed sheet pan and roast, stirring midway through cooking, until the eggplant is tender, about 20 minutes. Remove the vegetables from the oven and increase the oven temperature to 400°F.

4. While the vegetables cook, make the curry sauce: Combine the lemongrass, ginger, and the toasted coriander and cumin seeds in the bowl of a food processor and pulse to give it a rough chop. Add the lime zest, chiles, garlic, scallions, cilantro, remaining 2 tablespoons vegetable oil, and ¾ teaspoon salt. Pulse three or four times to chop, then process, pausing occasionally to scrape down the side of the bowl, until the mixture is well combined. It won't get smooth and creamy, but should be a rough-textured paste. Scrape the curry paste into a large bowl and whisk in the coconut milk. Set aside.

5. Place the puff pastry on a cutting board and prick it all over with a fork. Cut each sheet in half vertically, then into thirds horizontally so you have a total of 12 rectangles.

6. Remove the vegetables from the oven and transfer them to the bowl with the coconut curry, gently stirring to coat the vegetables with the sauce. Return the vegetables and sauce to the sheet pan, spreading them evenly across the entire surface.

7. Beginning at the left side of the sheet pan, place 2 pieces of puff pastry on top of the curry (with the long edge of the pastry parallel to the short side of the pan). Place another 2 pieces slightly overlapping the first 2. Continue, creating 2 rows with 6 rectangles in each row that slightly overlap. Brush the top of the pastry with melted butter.

8. Bake, rotating the sheet pan midway through cooking, until the pastry is puffed and golden brown, about 20 minutes. Remove from the oven and divide among bowls, making sure a piece or two of puff pastry sits atop each serving.

# THREE-CHEESE CRISPY MUSHROOM-PARM SANDWICH

*MAKES 4 SANDWICHES*

**E**ggplant is the usual go-to when it comes to a vegetarian-friendly parm sandwich, but eggplant really needs to be panfried in oil to get the texture and browned-ness that makes it taste so crisp and good when layered with the marinara and melted cheese. Mushrooms, however, can get a nice roast in the oven without frying and retain their juicy, meaty texture. To achieve the missing crunch component from the fried bread crumb coating, I toss panko bread crumbs with garlic oil, sprinkle them over the molten cheese, and crisp them under the broiler.

---

6 tablespoons extra-virgin olive oil
4 garlic cloves, grated on a
   Microplane-style rasp
⅓ cup panko bread crumbs
1 teaspoon plus a pinch of kosher salt
½ cup grated low-moisture
   mozzarella cheese
½ cup grated provolone cheese

¼ cup finely grated Parmigiano
   Reggiano cheese
4 portobello mushrooms, stemmed
   and sliced ¼ inch thick
½ cup favorite store-bought or
   homemade marinara sauce
4 sub rolls

---

1. Adjust an oven rack to the middle position and preheat the oven to 400°F.

2. Combine the olive oil and garlic in a ramekin and warm in the oven to infuse the oil, 5 minutes. (Alternatively, combine them in a microwave-safe bowl and microwave at high power until the garlic is fragrant, 30 to 45 seconds.) Pour 2 tablespoons garlic oil into a small bowl and add the panko bread crumbs and a pinch of salt. Rub this together with your fingers to combine and set aside (reserve the remaining garlic oil). In a separate small bowl combine the mozzarella, provolone, and Parmigiano Reggiano cheeses.

3. Place the mushrooms in a medium-size bowl and toss with 2 tablespoons garlic oil and the remaining 1 teaspoon salt. Transfer the mushrooms to a rimmed sheet

pan and roast until tender, 10 to 12 minutes (there's no need to flip them). Transfer the mushrooms to a plate and set aside. Line the sheet pan with aluminum foil.

4. Adjust an oven rack to the upper-middle position and preheat the broiler to high. Open the rolls and brush the interior of each half with some of the remaining garlic oil. Place the rolls, face up, on the prepared sheet pan and broil until the bread is golden brown, 2 to 3 minutes (watch the bread closely as broiler intensities vary). Remove the bread from the oven (keep the broiler on), divide the tops of the rolls among 4 plates, and leave the bottoms on the sheet pan.

5. Arrange the mushrooms over the bottom halves of the rolls and top each with 2 tablespoons marinara, spreading it out a bit. Divide the cheese over each mound of vegetables and return the sheet pan to the broiler. Broil until the cheese is melted, 2 to 3 minutes (watch the cheese closely so it does not burn). Sprinkle the reserved panko bread crumbs evenly over the cheese and return to the broiler until the crumbs are golden and crisp, 1 to 2 minutes. Transfer each portion to a plate and top with the reserved roll top. Serve hot.

# ROASTED POTATO AND POBLANO TACOS

(V) (GF) *MAKES 8 TACOS*

The idea behind these tacos is that the semi-spicy poblano and crisp potato filling are kept pretty basic so you taste their pure essence. After they are roasted to tender perfection, you stuff them into a warmed tortilla and top them with thoughtful and delicious add-ons for a variety of delicious, healthy, and fast tacos that are way more delicious than takeout (and drive-through, too!). Mix and match; try your own combos for endless taco night good times—and for even more taco bar ideas, see below! Fun.

2 medium-size Yukon Gold potatoes, chopped into bite-size pieces
2 large poblano peppers, halved, seeded, and chopped into bite-size pieces
2 tablespoons extra-virgin olive oil

1 teaspoon kosher salt
8 corn or flour tortillas (6-inch diameter)
Taco Truck Pickles (recipe follows; optional) and other toppings of choice (see below), for serving

1. Adjust an oven rack to the middle position, place a rimmed sheet pan on top, and preheat the oven to 400°F.

2. Toss the potatoes, poblanos, olive oil, and salt to coat in a medium-size bowl, then turn the mixture out onto the hot sheet pan. Roast, stirring occasionally, until the potatoes are browned and tender and the peppers are soft, 35 to 40 minutes. (I like how the peppers char a little from the hot pan; if you don't, start the potatoes first and add the peppers after 15 minutes.)

## Taco Bar Toppings!

Avocado slices or guacamole • Cooked black beans or pinto beans • Chopped fresh tomatoes mixed with chopped red onion, chopped fresh cilantro, salt, and fresh lime juice to taste • Chopped, pitted olives, mixed with roasted garlic • Crumbled Cotija or ricotta salata cheese • Fresh lime wedges • Fresh or frozen corn kernels blanched in hot water • Salsa, salsa, salsa! Red, green, with beans, or corn . . . It's all good and welcome. • Whole fresh cilantro leaves mixed with finely chopped white onion

3. Meanwhile, stack the tortillas in a double layer of damp paper towels and wrap loosely in aluminum foil. Place the tortillas in the oven until they are warmed through, 2 to 4 minutes.

4. Add some potatoes and poblanos to each warm tortilla (keep the unused ones wrapped in foil). Add toppings as desired and serve.

## VARIATIONS

Replace the potatoes and poblanos with any of the following vegetable combinations:

**Asparagus, Mushrooms, and Onions**
Combine 1 pound chopped asparagus, 8 ounces thinly sliced mushrooms, and 1 yellow onion, thinly sliced. Adjust the cook time to 20 minutes.

**Sweet Potatoes and Spinach**
Chop 2 sweet potatoes into bite-size pieces and roast until tender, 20 to 25 minutes. At the end of Step 2, toss with 3 cups roughly chopped spinach and return the pan to the oven just until the spinach wilts, 2 to 3 minutes.

**Rainbow Peppers and Radishes**
Combine 1 red bell pepper, 1 orange bell pepper, and 1 yellow bell pepper, each stemmed, seeded, and thinly sliced, with 8 ounces quartered radishes. Roast until tender, 20 to 25 minutes.

**Okra and Onions**
Toss together 1 pound okra, halved lengthwise, and 1 red onion, thinly sliced. Roast until the okra is crisp, about 25 minutes.

# TACO TRUCK PICKLES

MAKES ABOUT 1 PINT OF PICKLES (2 CUPS)

---

2 cups distilled white vinegar
1 tablespoon sugar
1 tablespoon kosher salt
8 ounces radishes, thinly sliced

4 ounces jalapeño peppers, stemmed (seeded for reduced heat, if you like) and thinly sliced

---

Combine the vinegar, sugar, and salt with 1 cup water in a large saucepan and bring to a boil over high heat. Add the radishes and jalapeños, return to a simmer, and turn off the heat. Set aside for 15 minutes. Divide the pickles among glass jars, cover with the brine, and refrigerate. The pickles will keep for 2 to 3 weeks.

# TORTILLA ROJO BAKE

(GF) *SERVES 6*

I t's one-half lasagna, one-half lazy enchiladas and one hundred percent so, so good. Instead of wrapping vegetables inside each tortilla and then bathing them in sauce and a blanket of cheese, I layer the tortillas lasagna-style with sheet pan–cooked cabbage, poblanos, mushrooms, and onions, add some cheese (you don't have to), and the sweet, smoky pureed red chile rojo sauce. Use the Charred Tomatillo Salsa (page 16), too, if you prefer, or your favorite purchased enchilada-style sauce.

---

6 cups very thinly sliced napa cabbage
1 red onion, halved and thinly sliced
8 ounces mushrooms, stemmed, caps thinly sliced
1 serrano or jalapeño chile, stemmed (seeded for reduced heat, if you like) and thinly sliced crosswise
3 garlic cloves, thinly sliced
3 tablespoons extra-virgin olive oil
1½ teaspoons kosher salt
½ teaspoon freshly ground black pepper

18 corn tortillas (6-inches each)
2¾ cups Guajillo Chile Sauce (page 183)
3 cups shredded Mexican cheese blend or a combination of mozzarella and Monterey Jack cheeses (optional)
4 scallions, thinly sliced
¾ cup crumbled Cotija cheese (optional)
½ cup roughly chopped fresh cilantro leaves

---

1. Adjust an oven rack to the middle position, place a rimmed jelly roll–size sheet pan on it, and preheat the oven to 400°F.

2. Place the cabbage, red onion, mushrooms, chile, and garlic in a large bowl. Add the olive oil, salt, and pepper and toss to combine. Turn the vegetables out onto the hot sheet pan and roast, stirring every 10 minutes, until the mushrooms are browned, 25 to 35 minutes. Transfer the vegetables to a heatproof bowl and save the sheet pan for Step 4 (no need to wash it).

3. Meanwhile, warm the tortillas directly over a gas burner set to medium heat, turning occasionally, or in a dry skillet over medium-high heat, turning occasionally, until the tortilla just starts to blister and becomes more pliable, 30 to 45 seconds per side. (I like how the edges get a little charred, but you can also stack the tortillas in 2 piles, wrap each in a damp paper towel followed

by a sheet of aluminum foil, and place them in the oven until warmed through, 5 to 8 minutes.)

4. Spread about ½ cup sauce over the bottom of the sheet pan in a thin, even layer. Lay the tortillas in the pan, overlapping them slightly. Cover with one-third of the vegetables, spreading them in an even layer. Spoon ¾ cup sauce over the vegetables, spreading it out as best you can with the back of a spoon. Cover with 1 cup shredded cheese (if using). Repeat 2 times with 2 more layers of tortillas, vegetables, sauce, and shredded cheese.

5. Bake until the cheese melts, 15 to 20 minutes. If not using cheese, bake until the tortillas are warmed through and the top layer of sauce looks dry, about 15 minutes. Remove from the oven and serve sprinkled with scallions, Cotija (if using), and cilantro.

# TOFU PUTTANESCA WITH GARLIC BREAD

(V) *SERVES 4*

**W**hen it's cold out and I crave something warm and comforting, this is the kind of food I turn to. Saucy, rich, and so, so satisfying. The tomato sauce is essentially roasted on the sheet pan, then you stir in the ingredients that give puttanesca its zing—crushed red pepper flakes, olives, and capers—before nestling slabs of tofu right into the sauce like you might do with chicken or fish. Tofu is kind of like a blank canvas for sauce—it doesn't contribute flavor or juiciness, but it has such a wonderful texture and heartiness, making it a great partner with this extra-bold, sharp, and piquant sauce. The garlic bread is an absolute necessity here— it's so good for sopping up all that wonderfully concentrated ragù.

**FOR THE PUTTANESCA**
6 medium-size tomatoes (as ripe as
  possible), cut into 1-inch pieces
3 garlic cloves, minced
1 medium-size yellow onion,
  finely chopped
1 large red bell pepper, stemmed,
  seeded, and thinly sliced
1 tablespoon finely chopped fresh
  rosemary leaves
2 tablespoons extra-virgin olive oil
2 teaspoons kosher salt
1 teaspoon freshly ground black
  pepper
¼ cup tomato paste
½ teaspoon crushed red pepper
  flakes
¾ cup fruity red wine, such as merlot
¾ cup halved pitted Kalamata olives

¼ cup capers, rinsed
1 brick (about 14 ounces) extra-firm
  tofu, drained and sliced lengthwise
  into 4 slabs
12 fresh basil leaves, stacked, rolled,
  and thinly sliced crosswise into
  ribbons

**FOR THE GARLIC BREAD**
4 tablespoons unsalted butter
  (or non-dairy butter)
2 tablespoons extra-virgin olive oil
2 garlic cloves, minced
¼ teaspoon kosher salt
1 baguette or rustic Italian loaf,
  halved crosswise and then
  lengthwise into 4 pieces
Sweet paprika, for sprinkling

1. Adjust an oven rack to the middle position and preheat the oven to 375°F.

2. To make the puttanesca: Toss the tomatoes, garlic, onion, red bell pepper, rosemary, olive oil,

1 teaspoon salt, and the pepper together in a large bowl. Turn the vegetables out onto a rimmed sheet pan and cover tightly with aluminum foil. Bake until the vegetables start to soften and become tender, about 20 minutes.

3. Remove the sheet pan from the oven and remove the foil. (Save it—you'll use it again.) With a rubber spatula, smash and stir the tomatoes into the other ingredients. Add the tomato paste and crushed red pepper flakes, stirring them in. Stir in the wine, olives, capers, and remaining teaspoon salt. Nestle the tofu into the sauce, leaving space between so all sides are exposed to the sauce. Spoon some sauce over the top. Place the foil over the pan again and bake until the tofu is heated through, about 20 minutes. Remove from the oven and set aside, covered.

4. To make the garlic bread: While the tofu cooks, combine the butter, olive oil, garlic, and salt in a microwave-safe bowl. Microwave at high power for 1 minute, swirling every 20 seconds, until the butter is melted and incorporated. Brush or spoon the garlic butter over the cut sides of the bread. Sprinkle with a few dashes of paprika. Line a rimmed sheet pan with parchment paper and place the bread, butter-side up, on top (or just broil the bread on a sheet of foil).

5. Adjust an oven rack to the upper-middle position and preheat the broiler to high. Broil the bread until it is sizzling and golden brown, 1 to 3 minutes (watch the bread closely as broiler intensities vary). Remove the bread from the oven and divide it among 4 plates. Divide the tofu and sauce among the plates and serve sprinkled with basil.

# SUMMER TOMATO SLAB PIE WITH FLAKY SAGE CRUST

*SERVES ABOUT 8*

What else is there to say but "delicious"? I am from the Midwest and never heard of tomato pie until I was writing about a Southern chef's favorite take on one. . . . I made it and then was totally hooked. It's kind of like a quiche, but a little tangier and homier. (So don't worry if your crust doesn't look Pinterest worthy—imperfection is all part of this rustic tart's charm.) Of course, it's called a slab pie because this bad boy isn't served in slices—it's lifted out from the pan in sheets! Note that this recipe does take a bit of time to make . . . but I promise it's well worth the effort and you'll bask in the accolades. Of course, if you want to plan ahead, you can make the crust up to two days in advance and refrigerate it either as a rectangle (Step 1) or rolled out and fitted into the pan (Step 2); or freeze it, wrapped well in plastic, for up to 2 months. You'll need a 10 x 16-inch jelly-roll pan for this recipe.

---

## FOR THE SAGE CRUST

½ cup fresh sage leaves, roughly chopped
2 garlic cloves, roughly chopped
Zest of 1 lemon
1½ teaspoons kosher salt
½ teaspoon freshly ground black pepper
2⅔ cups all-purpose flour
¾ cup whole-wheat flour
1½ tablespoons sugar
2½ sticks (10 ounces) cold unsalted butter
½ cup ice water

## FOR THE TOMATO FILLING

1 cup mayonnaise
1 cup buttermilk
2 large eggs
1 cup finely grated Parmigiano Reggiano cheese
1 teaspoon fresh lemon juice
½ teaspoon kosher salt
½ teaspoon freshly ground black pepper
4 scallions, thinly sliced
1 cup finely chopped fresh basil leaves
2 cups tomatoes (quartered if large, halved if using cherry tomatoes or other small tomatoes)

---

1. To make the crust: In the bowl of a food processor combine the sage, garlic, lemon zest, salt, and pepper and pulse until the sage is finely chopped, four or five (1-second) pulses. Add the all-purpose flour, whole-wheat flour, and sugar and process until well combined. Add the butter and pulse until there aren't any butter pieces larger than a small pea, about ten (1-second) pulses. Add the ice water, 1 tablespoon at a time, pulsing once between each addition, until you can squeeze the dough in your palm without it falling apart, about eight pulses in all. Turn the dough out onto a large sheet of plastic wrap and press it into a 1-inch-thick rectangle. Wrap it in plastic and refrigerate for at least 30 minutes, or up to 2 days.

2. Place the chilled dough on a sheet of parchment paper (or plastic wrap) and put another piece on top. Roll the dough into an 11 x 17 x ½-inch-thick rectangle (it should be just a tad bigger than the size of your sheet pan). Remove the parchment from the top and flip the dough onto a rimmed jelly roll–size sheet pan. Peel away the other sheet of parchment (save it for Step 3) and adjust the dough so it fits into the edges of the pan. Fold the edges of the dough over and pinch, crimp, or press down on them with the tines of a fork to make a decorative edge.

3. Refrigerate the dough in the sheet pan for 30 minutes, or freeze for 15 minutes. If you plan to let the dough rest longer, cover the sheet pan with plastic wrap. Adjust one oven rack to the upper-middle position and another to the lower-middle position. Preheat the oven to 400°F.

4. Line the dough with the reserved parchment paper (or aluminum foil) and top with pie weights or dried beans to weigh down the parchment. Bake the crust on the lower-middle rack until the edges are golden and the dough doesn't look shiny or raw when you lift the parchment, 20 to 25 minutes. Remove the crust from the oven, remove the parchment and pie weights, and set aside.

5. To make the filling: While the crust bakes, whisk the mayonnaise, buttermilk, eggs, ¾ cup Parmigiano Reggiano cheese, lemon juice, salt, and pepper in a large bowl. Stir in the scallions and basil and then pour the filling into the crust. Arrange the tomatoes on top. (I like them scattered and rustic looking.) Sprinkle the remaining ¼ cup cheese over the top and return the pie to the oven until the filling is golden brown and resists light pressure, 18 to 20 minutes.

6. Move the pie to the upper-middle rack and turn the broiler to high. Broil the pie until it blisters in spots, 1½ to 2 minutes (watch the pie closely as broiler intensities vary). Remove from the oven and cool for at least 30 minutes before slicing and serving.

# ZUCCHINI RIBBONS AGLIO E OLIO

(V) (GF)  *SERVES 4*

**"Z**oodles," or zucchini ribbon noodles, need a bare few minutes on a hot sheet pan to become al dente. This is an incredibly speedy dish that you can serve solo or as a "zoodle" salad by adding cubes of mozzarella, halved cherry tomatoes, blanched broccoli or cauliflower . . . You can even toss the cooked zucchini with store-bought pesto instead of the garlic oil.

If you don't have a spiralizer and your grocery store doesn't carry zoodles, you can slice the zucchini lengthwise into ¼-inch- to ⅛-inch-thick planks, stack the planks, and then slice them lengthwise again into long thin sticks.

---

2 tablespoons extra-virgin olive oil
3 garlic cloves, grated on a
    Microplane-style rasp
Heaping ¼ teaspoon crushed red
    pepper flakes
8 cups spiralized zucchini (from
    about 6 medium-size zucchini)

1 teaspoon kosher salt
Heaping ¼ cup fresh basil leaves,
    stacked, rolled, and very thinly
    sliced crosswise into ribbons
Flaky sea salt (or more kosher salt),
    for serving
¼ cup toasted pine nuts (optional)

---

1. Adjust an oven rack to the middle position, place a rimmed sheet pan on top, and preheat the oven to 475°F.

2. Place the oil, garlic, and crushed red pepper flakes in a small heatproof bowl (such as a ramekin) and place it in the oven until the garlic is fragrant, 2 to 3 minutes. Remove from the oven and set aside.

3. Place the zucchini on a rimmed sheet pan, add the garlic oil, and toss to coat. Roast until the zucchini is tender and golden, 5 to 7 minutes, stirring midway through cooking. (You don't want the zucchini to become deeply browned.)

4. Transfer the zucchini to a serving bowl and toss gently with the kosher salt. Sprinkle with the basil, flaky salt, and pine nuts (if using), and serve.

# Chapter 4

# GRAIN BOWLS AND BEYOND

**G**rains cooked on a sheet pan in the oven? Not only does this method work, but it *slays* it. The grains cook up fluffy and light and there is a wide margin for error because you can keep the grains in the oven for a few minutes too long (up to 10 minutes or so) without doing too much harm. (They'll be a little chewier and drier, but you won't have scorched grains stuck to the bottom of your pot as you would on the stovetop.) It couldn't be simpler—just stir boiling water or another liquid into the grains on the sheet pan, cover tightly with aluminum foil, and bake until fluffy. See page 114 for a simple grain chart—so even if you just need to make a side dish of rice or bulgur for your non–sheet pan dinner (*gasp!* is there such a thing?), you can turn to the handy chart for cooking times and temperatures. And for dinner tonight, check out the many options herein, from hearty vegetable-topped grain bowls to creamy polenta!

# MY GO-TO RICE AND BEANS WITH PICO DE GALLO

V  GF  *SERVES 4*

It seems like there are a million and one ways to make rice and beans . . . and here's one more that is super efficient because—surprise!—it's made all at once on a sheet pan. Making them on a sheet pan is super easy—essentially you're seasoning boiling water with spices, adding the rice *and* the beans, covering the sheet pan, and baking them in the oven. The rice cooks to a perfect fluffiness. The first time I made this, instead of making my own pico de gallo, I just stirred in some store-bought fresh salsa. You can do the same, or make my tasty pico (page 89) for a burst of fresh flavors. (If you opt for the latter, throw it together while the rice and beans bake.) This is a great kid-friendly dish that works with almost any array of vegetables or proteins, or served on its own as the centerpiece of your meal.

---

1½ teaspoons ground cumin
1 teaspoon ground coriander
1 teaspoon chili powder
1 teaspoon garlic powder
1 teaspoon sweet paprika
1 teaspoon kosher salt
½ teaspoon ancho chile powder or smoked paprika
½ teaspoon freshly ground black pepper

1½ cups long-grain white rice
1 can (15 ounces) black beans, drained and rinsed
1½ cups boiling water
1 cup vegetable broth
Pico de Gallo (recipe follows) for serving, or 1 cup store-bought salsa

---

1. Adjust an oven rack to the middle position and preheat the oven to 400°F.

2. Stir together the cumin, coriander, chili powder, garlic powder, paprika, salt, ancho chile powder, and pepper in a small bowl and sprinkle the mixture over the bottom of a rimmed sheet pan. Stir in the rice and black beans, then set the sheet pan on the oven rack. Pour in the boiling

water and vegetable broth, and stir to combine (the spices won't be perfectly incorporated, and that's okay).

3. Cover the sheet pan with aluminum foil (you may need 2 sheets), crimping it tightly around the edges of the pan to seal. Bake until the rice is fluffy and has absorbed all the liquid (carefully peek under one corner of the foil so not much steam escapes), about 25 minutes.

4. Remove the pan from the oven and let it stand, covered, for 5 minutes. Then carefully remove and discard the aluminum foil. Transfer the rice and beans to a large bowl. Add the pico de gallo and stir with a fork to fluff until combined. Serve warm or at room temperature.

# PICO DE GALLO

(V) (GF) *MAKES ABOUT 1 CUP*

---

1 large tomato, cored and finely chopped
1 small red onion, finely chopped
½ jalapeño chile, stemmed (seeded to reduce heat, if you like) and finely chopped

½ cup finely chopped fresh cilantro leaves
Juice of 1 lime
½ teaspoon kosher salt

---

Stir together the tomato, red onion, jalapeño, cilantro, lime juice, and salt in a small bowl and set it aside. It will keep, refrigerated in an airtight container, for 2 days.

# QUINOA AND SWEET POTATO BOWL WITH TAHINI-MISO DRESSING AND SUNFLOWER SEEDS

(V) (GF) *SERVES 4*

Grain bowls—they have taken over the universe! Healthy, filling, and loaded with veggies, they're more substantial than a salad and offer all the nuance, texture, and flavor balance of a great sandwich (minus the bread). Grain bowls beg for creativity—when I make one, I always strive to hit savory-sweet-salty-spicy-crunchy-creamy-cold-warm-herby-citrusy-chewy in every bite. (Okay fine, maybe every other bite.) Here, sweet potatoes give fluffy quinoa some substance, while a very creamy tahini and miso dressing enriches this otherwise lean bowl. Chopped fresh spinach, crunchy sunflower seeds, chopped jalapeño, and scallions add texture, heat, and sharpness, offering loads of flavor and contrast each time you dive in for another forkful.

---

3 medium-size sweet potatoes, peeled or unpeeled, quartered lengthwise, and cut crosswise into ¾-inch pieces

¼ cup extra-virgin olive oil

¾ teaspoon kosher salt, plus extra as needed

1½ cups quinoa, rinsed well

2 cups boiling water

4 cups fresh baby spinach

2 limes

¼ cup tahini (sesame paste; see page 26)

2 tablespoons white miso paste (see Note, page 24)

1 tablespoon plus 1 teaspoon soy sauce

¼ cup almond, soy, or cow's milk

1 cup fresh cilantro leaves, finely chopped

1 serrano or jalapeño chile, stemmed (seeded for reduced heat, if you like) and finely chopped

4 scallions, ends trimmed, white and light green parts thinly sliced on a diagonal

¼ cup roasted, salted sunflower seeds

---

1. Adjust an oven rack to the middle position and preheat the oven to 350°F.

2. Toss the sweet potatoes with 2 tablespoons olive oil and ½ teaspoon salt in a medium-size bowl. Turn the potatoes out onto a rimmed sheet pan and roast until they begin to soften, about 15 minutes.

3. Wearing oven mitts, remove the sheet pan from the oven and add the quinoa. Pull the oven rack out partway, place the pan back on it, and carefully add the boiling water. Give everything a quick stir to disperse the potatoes, quinoa, and water evenly, and cover the sheet pan with aluminum foil (you may need 2 sheets), crimping it tightly around the edges to seal. Bake for 10 minutes. Uncover the pan, stir the quinoa, re-cover the pan, and bake until all the water is absorbed, about 10 minutes more. Remove the pan from the oven and set it aside, covered.

4. While the quinoa bakes, make the toppings: Place the spinach in a medium-size bowl and toss with the remaining 2 tablespoons olive oil and ¼ teaspoon salt. Juice the limes into a small bowl. Add half the juice to the spinach, tossing to combine. To the remaining lime juice, add the tahini and miso and whisk until smooth. Add the soy sauce and almond milk and whisk again until smooth. Taste and add a pinch of salt if needed. Stir in the cilantro and chopped jalapeño.

5. Divide the quinoa mixture among 4 bowls and top each with the dressed spinach and some scallions. Divide the tahini-miso dressing evenly over the top, sprinkle with the sunflower seeds, and serve.

## A Safety Note

It does take a bit of care when it comes to adding hot water to a hot pan so you don't burn yourself with the liquid or accidentally touch the inside of the oven. My technique is to pull the oven rack out halfway, place the grain-filled sheet pan on it, add the hot water, carefully lay the foil over the pan, crimp it around the edges (if the pan is hot, wear oven mitts to protect your hands), carefully slide the rack back into the oven, and close the door. You want this to happen as quickly as possible so you don't lose too much oven heat, so keep that in mind as well. Your first few times, you may consider jacking the oven temperature 50°F higher than the recipe calls for so that by the time you shut the oven door, the oven will be at or near the right temperature (remember to decrease the set oven temp on the oven dial, too!).

# QUINOA AND TOFU BOWL WITH ARUGULA AND CREAMY CILANTRO DRESSING

(V) (GF) *SERVES 4*

In this quinoa bowl—technically quinoa is a seed, not a grain, but a seed bowl just has less appeal, right?—the onion and bell pepper get a head start roasting on the sheet pan to caramelize and brown, then the quinoa is stirred in, and everything finishes cooking together in the oven. A creamy, cilantro-spiked, dairy-free cashew dressing is a rich, herby topper to the quinoa base, while the arugula is used almost like an herb for a fresh, peppery flavor. This cashew-cilantro dressing is so good you may want to make extra for dressing pasta, boiled potatoes, a simple green salad . . . just about anything!

---

2 cups raw cashews
1¼ cups cold water
3 tablespoons extra-virgin olive oil
1 medium-size red onion, finely chopped
1 small red bell pepper, stemmed, seeded, and finely chopped
12 ounces (about 2 packages) baked tofu, cut crosswise into ¼-inch-thick planks
3 teaspoons kosher salt, plus extra as needed
1½ cups quinoa, rinsed well

2 cups boiling water
¼ cup finely chopped fresh cilantro leaves
1 garlic clove, roughly chopped
½ jalapeño chile, stemmed (seeded for reduced heat, if you like) and roughly chopped (optional)
¼ teaspoon freshly ground black pepper
4 cups arugula, roughly chopped
½ lime

---

1. Adjust an oven rack to the middle position, place a rimmed sheet pan on the rack, and preheat the oven to 350°F.

2. Place the cashews in a medium-size bowl and add the cold water. Let the cashews soak for 15 minutes, stirring halfway through soaking.

3. Combine 2 tablespoons olive oil with the red onion, red bell pepper, tofu, and ¾ teaspoon salt on the sheet pan and spread it into an even layer. Cook until the onion and tofu begin to brown, about 20 minutes.

4. Wearing oven mitts, remove the sheet pan from the oven and add the quinoa, sprinkling it evenly over the tofu mixture. Pull the oven rack out partway, place the pan back on it, and carefully pour the boiling water evenly over the top. Cover the sheet pan with aluminum foil (you may need 2 sheets), crimping it tightly around the edges to seal. Bake for 10 minutes. Carefully uncover the pan and stir the quinoa. Re-cover the pan and bake until all the water is absorbed, about 10 minutes more. Remove the pan from the oven and set it aside, covered.

5. While the quinoa bakes, make the dressing: Transfer the cashews and their soaking liquid to a blender. Add the cilantro, garlic, jalapeño (if using), 2 teaspoons salt, and pepper. Blend until the mixture is very creamy and smooth, 45 seconds to 1 minute. If you'd like the dressing thinner, add more water. Taste and adjust the salt if needed.

6. Place the arugula in a medium-size bowl and toss with the remaining tablespoon olive oil and ¼ teaspoon salt. Squeeze the lime half over the top and toss to combine.

7. Divide the quinoa mixture among 4 bowls. Scooch some of it to the side to make room for a mound of arugula. Drizzle the dressing over the top and serve.

## Grain Bowls to Go

Grain bowls don't just make a wonderful, healthy, and delicious dinner; they can also be that perfect take-along meal—for a long flight, lunch at the office, or a day of sports activities. (Why depend on fast food or pizza for sustenance between soccer practice and gymnastics?) You can premix them with the dressing and pack them into airtight containers or Mason jars and sprinkle the crunchy component (seeds, nuts, chopped undressed salad greens, or herbs) over the top before putting on the lid.

# FORBIDDEN RICE BOWL WITH BEETS AND GOAT CHEESE–DILL VINAIGRETTE

**GF** *SERVES 4*

**D**ark, stark, and beautiful—black "forbidden" rice is a statement grain. It cooks up with the hearty chew of brown rice, but has a more floral, less nutty flavor (it's available in most health-minded grocery stores or in the organic aisle of the supermarket). Here, I roast beets and red onion on a sheet pan before adding the black rice, which ends up staining the vegetables inky black. It's very *noir*—a bit moody, yet pleasantly sweet when you bite into a beet or red onion, both of which are naturally sweeter than their yellow counterparts. The goat cheese–and-dill vinaigrette offers a classic flavor pairing for the beets, while the pistachios add crunch and that gorgeous bright green burst of color.

---

3 medium-size beets, peeled and cut into bite-size pieces (see box, page 96)

1 small red onion, halved and thinly sliced

6 tablespoons extra-virgin olive oil

1¾ teaspoons kosher salt, plus extra as needed

1½ cups black rice (see headnote)

3 cups boiling water

2¼ cups (about 8 ounces) thinly sliced red cabbage

3 tablespoons plus 2 teaspoons fresh lemon juice

2 tablespoons chopped fresh dill

2 teaspoons honey

½ teaspoon freshly ground black pepper, plus extra as needed

4 ounces fresh goat cheese

¼ cup shelled, roasted, salted pistachios

---

**1.** Adjust an oven rack to the middle position and preheat the oven to 350°F.

**2.** Place the beets and red onion onto a rimmed sheet pan and toss with 2 tablespoons olive oil and 1 teaspoon salt. Roast until they start to soften, about 15 minutes.

3. Wearing oven mitts, remove the pan from the oven and add the rice, sprinkling it evenly over the beet mixture. Pull the oven rack out partway, place the pan back on it, carefully add the boiling water, and give everything a quick stir to distribute evenly. Cover the sheet pan with aluminum foil (you may need 2 sheets), crimping it tightly around the edges to seal. Bake until the rice is tender and the water is evaporated, 35 to 45 minutes. Remove the sheet pan from the oven and set it aside (leave it covered).

4. While the rice bakes, place the cabbage in a medium-size bowl and massage it with 1 tablespoon oil, 2 teaspoons lemon juice, and ¼ teaspoon salt, and set it aside.

5. Whisk 3 tablespoons olive oil with the remaining 3 tablespoons lemon juice, dill, honey, ½ teaspoon salt, and pepper in a small bowl. Crumble in the goat cheese and stir gently. Taste and add more salt or pepper if needed.

6. Divide the rice among 4 bowls. Top with the cabbage and some goat cheese vinaigrette. Sprinkle the pistachios over the top before serving.

## Peeling—Not Wearing—Beets

Pink-stained fingertips are the telltale sign of a beet lover. To protect your hands, you can wear kitchen gloves or latex gloves when peeling beets, or hold the beet with a paper towel while you peel it.

# BROWN RICE BOWL WITH MAPLE-ROASTED PARSNIPS, FENNEL, DATES, AND SPICY PUMPKIN SEEDS

(V) (GF)  *SERVES 4*

Here parsnips are roasted until caramelized and spoon-tender, then finished with maple syrup for a hint of sweetness that works beautifully against the spicy earthiness of the pumpkin seeds and the slight citrusy sweetness of the orange-mint vinaigrette. You could totally use any kind of root vegetable instead, from carrots to rutabaga, radishes, turnips, and kohlrabi, or a wonderful root-y medley of everything.

---

## FOR THE SPICY PUMPKIN SEEDS

¼ teaspoon ground cinnamon
⅛ teaspoon ground allspice
⅛ teaspoon cayenne pepper
⅛ teaspoon smoked paprika
⅛ teaspoon kosher salt
1 teaspoon extra-virgin olive oil
⅓ cup pumpkin seeds (pepitas)

## FOR THE RICE BOWL

3 medium-size parsnips, trimmed, peeled, and quartered lengthwise
3 medium-size shallots, halved and thinly sliced

6 tablespoons extra-virgin olive oil
1¼ teaspoons kosher salt
1 tablespoon maple syrup
1½ cups long-grain brown rice
3 cups boiling water
½ cup pitted, chopped dates
3 tablespoons fresh orange juice
2 tablespoons rice vinegar
¼ cup finely chopped fresh mint leaves
1 fennel bulb, stalks removed, halved, cored, and thinly sliced (chop some fronds for serving, optional)

---

1. Adjust an oven rack to the middle position and preheat the oven to 400°F.

2. To make the spicy pumpkin seeds: Whisk the cinnamon, allspice, cayenne, paprika, and salt in a small bowl. Stir in the olive oil until combined. Add the pumpkin seeds

and toss to coat. Turn the seeds out onto a small square of aluminum foil, transfer the foil to a rimmed sheet pan, and toast the seeds in the oven until they are slightly puffed looking and fragrant, about 8 minutes. Remove from the pan and set aside.

3. To make the rice bowls: Place the parsnips and shallots in a medium-size bowl and toss with 2 tablespoons olive oil and 1 teaspoon salt. Turn them out onto the rimmed sheet pan and roast until tender, 17 to 20 minutes. Transfer the vegetables to a large plate and toss with the maple syrup; reserve the sheet pan. Reduce the oven temperature to 350°F.

4. Wearing oven mitts, add the rice to the sheet pan, spreading it in an even layer. Pull the oven rack out partway, place the pan back on it, carefully add the boiling water, and sprinkle in the dates. Cover the sheet

pan with aluminum foil (you may need 2 sheets), crimping it tightly around the edges to seal. Bake until the rice is tender and the water is evaporated, 35 to 40 minutes. Remove the sheet pan from the oven and set it aside (keep it covered).

5. Whisk the remaining ¼ cup olive oil with the orange juice, rice vinegar, and remaining ¼ teaspoon salt in a small bowl. Reserve 2 tablespoons and pour the rest over the rice. Add the mint and fluff the mixture with a fork.

6. Divide the rice among 4 bowls. Place the sliced fennel in a small bowl, add the reserved vinaigrette, and toss to combine. Top each rice bowl with equal amounts of fennel. Divide the parsnips and shallots among the bowls and garnish with the spiced pumpkin seeds and fennel fronds (if using).

# I CAN'T BELIEVE IT'S MUSHROOM RISOTTO!

**GF** *SERVES 4*

Um, wait. Risotto on a sheet pan? Uh, yeah! The oven's heat is very gentle, meaning you *don't* have to stir the rice constantly (as you do when making it on the stovetop) since there is such a small chance of scorching the risotto; essentially all you need to do is add liquid and stir every 5 minutes or so. Plus you free up precious stovetop space for other pursuits, whatever those may be. Sheet pan risotto is only as delicious as your broth is—make your own (page 112) or buy the best quality broth you can find.

---

8 ounces mushrooms (such as cremini, shiitake, maitake, porcini, chanterelle, or portobello), trimmed and quartered (cut portobellos or other large mushrooms into bite-size pieces)

1 small red onion, finely chopped

3 garlic cloves, minced

3 tablespoons extra-virgin olive oil

½ teaspoon kosher salt, plus extra as needed

½ cup dry white wine

1¼ cups arborio rice

4½ cups boiling vegetable broth (or equal parts broth and water)

3 tablespoons unsalted butter, at room temperature

½ cup finely grated Parmigiano Reggiano cheese

Freshly ground black pepper

¼ cup finely chopped fresh flat-leaf parsley leaves or fresh basil leaves

---

1. Adjust an oven rack to the middle position and preheat the oven to 400°F.

2. Place the mushrooms, red onion, garlic, olive oil, and salt in a medium-size bowl and toss to combine. Turn the mixture out onto a rimmed sheet pan and roast, stirring midway through cooking, until the mushrooms are browned, about 20 minutes.

3. Stir the wine into the mushroom mixture and return the pan to the oven for 5 minutes. Wearing oven mitts, pull the oven rack out partway and stir in the rice. Slide the rack back into place and continue to bake for 5 minutes.

4. Pull out the oven rack partway again and stir in 1¼ cups broth into the rice. Carefully slide the rack back into place and bake until the

liquid is mostly absorbed, about 8 minutes. Pull out the oven rack partway and stir in another 1¼ cups broth. Carefully slide the rack back into place and bake for 5 minutes more (the rice will start to look more cooked and starchier). Pull the rack out partway once more and carefully stir in 1 cup broth. Bake 5 minutes, then stir in the remaining cup of broth. Bake until the rice is no longer opaque and is tender yet slightly al dente, about 5 minutes more (total cooking time after stirring in the first addition of broth is about 25 minutes).

5. Stir in the butter followed by the Parmigiano Reggiano cheese. Taste and add salt and pepper as needed. Stir in most of the parsley and sprinkle a little over the top before serving.

# BULGUR BOWL WITH NAPA CABBAGE, MELTED RED ONIONS, AND ALMONDS

**VO** *SERVES 4*

**W**hat I love about bulgur is how quickly it cooks in the oven. It always comes out plump and pleasantly toothsome—there really are no worries about soggy bulgur, which can happen when it is cooked on the stovetop. You get crunch from the almonds, sweet caramelized goodness from the onion and cabbage, and brightness from the lemon juice. The cardamom-honey vinaigrette is just exotic enough, transforming this fairly economical bowl into something that tastes restaurant special.

---

1 medium-size red onion, halved and thinly sliced
½ small head napa cabbage, cored and sliced into ½-inch strips (about 4 cups)
6 tablespoons extra-virgin olive oil
1¼ teaspoons kosher salt
½ cup golden raisins
1 cup bulgur

2 cups boiling water
½ cup slivered almonds
2 tablespoons fresh lemon juice
1½ teaspoons maple syrup or honey
1 teaspoon ground cardamom
1 teaspoon ground coriander
¼ teaspoon freshly ground black pepper

---

1. Adjust an oven rack to the middle position and preheat the oven to 400°F.

2. Combine the red onion and cabbage in a large bowl and toss with 3 tablespoons olive oil and ½ teaspoon salt. Turn the mixture out onto a rimmed sheet pan, spread into an even layer, and cook until the cabbage begins to brown around the edges and the onions are tender, about 25 minutes. Stir in the raisins and cook for 5 minutes more. Transfer the vegetables to a bowl and reduce the oven temperature to 350°F.

3. Add the bulgur to the sheet pan (no need to clean it), pull the oven rack out partway, and place the pan on it. Carefully add the boiling water

and ¼ teaspoon salt. Give the bulgur a quick stir and spread it into an even layer. Wearing oven mitts, cover the sheet pan with aluminum foil (you may need 2 sheets), crimping it tightly around the edges to seal. Bake until the bulgur is tender and the water is absorbed, about 10 minutes. Remove the sheet pan from the oven and set it aside, covered, for 10 minutes.

4. While the bulgur cooks, place the almonds on another rimmed sheet pan or on a square of aluminum foil and toast in the oven until golden brown, about 8 minutes.

5. Meanwhile, make the vinaigrette: Whisk together the remaining 3 tablespoons olive oil, lemon juice, honey, cardamom, coriander, pepper, and remaining ½ teaspoon salt in a small bowl.

6. Transfer the bulgur to a large bowl. Drizzle the vinaigrette over it and fluff the bulgur with a fork. Add the roasted vegetables and toss to combine. Divide among 4 bowls, sprinkle the toasted almonds on top, and serve.

## Transform Your Cooking in a Pinch (or a Spoonful)

We all get stuck in a cooking rut sometimes. You get tired of making the same old thing and, sometimes, with work schedules and the demands of life, it's hard to break out of your cooking routine. I'm here to tell you it's actually *easy*—when you count on an unusual spice, spice blend, herb, or ingredient to pull you through.

For example, cardamom. Cardamom is a little grassy, a little musky, a little spicy. . . . It's exotic and gorgeous in both savory and sweet foods, plus you can swap it for cinnamon in just about any recipe and, *snap*, just like that, you gave your morning toast a breath of the Far East! Lemongrass is another great ingredient to play with. Instead of a bay leaf, add a smashed lemongrass stalk to a sauce or broth for a soft, citrusy flavor. Here are some other fun ingredient swaps—get to know these players and bring a whole new feel to your favorite meal!

| INSTEAD OF . . . | TRY |
| --- | --- |
| Basil (fresh) | Fresh cilantro mixed with fresh mint |
| Bay leaf | Lemongrass (smashed) |
| Butter | Coconut oil |
| Cinnamon (ground) | Cardamom (ground) |
| Crushed red pepper flakes | Smoked paprika (pimenton) |
| Flaky salt | Smoked salt |
| Honey | Pomegranate molasses |
| Hot sauce or Sriracha | Gochujang (Korean red chile paste) |
| Lime juice (fresh) | Bottled yuzu juice (available in Asian markets) |
| Maple syrup | Date syrup |
| Parmigiano Reggiano cheese | Cashew-miso spread (page 73) |
| Peanut butter | Sesame paste (tahini) |
| Peanuts | Sunflower seeds |
| Sweet paprika | Turmeric (ground) |
| Water | Herb broth (page 113) |
| White wine vinegar | Rice vinegar |

# HERBY SINGED-TOMATO TABOULI

(V) SERVES 4

**W**hat makes this tabouli special is the singed tomatoes—they add a juicy dimension and a hint of char to this otherwise supremely fresh assembly of very-good-for-you ingredients. The key to great tabouli is loads of fresh herbs. If you have a giant bunch of parsley or mint, add more than called for here! I love the crunch and roasted taste the sunflower seeds add to this classic Middle Eastern dish. You can also make this with quinoa instead of bulgur for a gluten-free version. Increase the amount of water to 1 cup and cook the quinoa for an extra 10 minutes, stirring midway through cooking.

---

3 plum tomatoes, cored and chopped into ½-inch pieces

¼ cup extra-virgin olive oil

¾ teaspoon kosher salt, plus extra as needed

¾ cup bulgur

¾ cup boiling water

½ small red onion, finely chopped

1 large cucumber, finely chopped (peeled or unpeeled)

⅔ cup finely chopped fresh flat-leaf parsley leaves

½ cup finely chopped fresh mint leaves

1 tablespoon finely chopped fresh chives or scallions

Juice of ½ lemon, plus extra as needed

¼ teaspoon freshly ground black pepper

2 tablespoons roasted, salted sunflower seeds

---

1. Adjust an oven rack to the top position and preheat the broiler to high.

2. Place the tomatoes in a large bowl with 2 tablespoons olive oil and ½ teaspoon salt and toss to combine. Turn the tomatoes out onto a rimmed sheet pan and broil until they start to blacken in spots, about 8 minutes (watch the tomatoes closely as broiler intensities vary). Remove the sheet pan and reduce the oven temperature to 350°F.

3. Wearing oven mitts, pull the oven rack out partway, place the sheet pan on it, and carefully stir the bulgur and boiling water into the tomatoes; spread the mixture out evenly. Cover

the sheet pan with aluminum foil (you may need 2 sheets), crimping it tightly around the edges to seal. Bake until the bulgur absorbs all (or nearly all) the liquid, about 10 minutes (carefully peek under a corner of the foil to check). Remove the pan from the oven and set it aside, covered, for 10 minutes.

4. Place the red onion in a small bowl and toss with the remaining ¼ teaspoon salt. Set it aside.

5. Scrape the bulgur mixture into a large bowl and fluff it with a fork. Add the salted red onion, cucumber, parsley, mint, chives, lemon juice, pepper, and remaining 2 tablespoons olive oil. Stir to combine and taste, adjusting the flavor with more lemon juice or salt if needed. Serve sprinkled with sunflower seeds.

# CREAMY CARROT POLENTA WITH WINTER SQUASH RAGÙ

**VO** **GF** *SERVES 4*

Polenta may sound fancy, but it is really no more than coarsely ground dried corn kernels, also known as grits. To add extra nutrition and flavor, I stir carrot juice into the cooking liquid. It naturally sweetens the polenta and also lends its happy orange color to the dish. The polenta cooks up solid but not firm, so it's easy to transfer to a bowl and whisk in some butter and Parmigiano Reggiano cheese for extra creaminess. This makes a fantastic side dish or base to any stew-y topper. Here, I serve it with a saucy tomato-enriched winter squash ragù made with rosemary and white wine. The result is a hearty, comforting bowl that makes me want to tuck into it while curled up in front of a proverbial fireplace with a good book.

For a vegan version, simply substitute non-dairy butter and leave out the cheese (or use vegan cheese).

---

1 pound winter squash, peeled, seeded, and chopped into bite-size pieces
8 ounces brown mushrooms, trimmed and quartered
1 small yellow onion, finely chopped
3 tablespoons extra-virgin olive oil
1¼ teaspoons kosher salt
2 large tomatoes, cored and chopped
4 garlic cloves, minced
1 tablespoon finely chopped fresh rosemary leaves

½ cup dry white wine
1½ cups carrot juice (see box, page 112)
2 cups boiling water
1¼ cups medium-grind stone-ground cornmeal
3 tablespoons unsalted butter, at room temperature
¼ cup finely grated Parmigiano Reggiano cheese

---

1. Adjust an oven rack to the middle position and preheat the oven to 450°F.

2. Place the squash, mushrooms, onion, 2 tablespoons olive oil, and 1 teaspoon salt in a medium-size bowl and toss to combine. Turn the

vegetables out onto a rimmed sheet pan (reserve the bowl), spread them into an even layer, and roast for 15 minutes.

3. Place the tomatoes, garlic, rosemary, remaining tablespoon olive oil, and ¼ teaspoon salt in the previously used bowl and toss to combine.

4. Pull the oven rack out partway, place the sheet pan on it, and carefully add the wine and the seasoned tomatoes to the squash mixture, stirring to combine. Reduce the oven temperature to 350°F and roast until the tomatoes break down and the mixture is very juicy, 15 to 20 minutes. Transfer the squash ragù

back to the bowl (don't wipe out the pan).

5. Return the sheet pan to the oven rack. Carefully add the carrot juice and boiling water. With a fork, stir in the cornmeal a little at a time so there aren't any lumps and spread the cornmeal into an even layer. (It won't cook in an even layer but that's okay—it will all be cooked through.) Bake, uncovered, until the polenta is set, about 20 minutes. (It may still be a little loose in the corners if the liquid pooled to one side of the sheet pan.)

6. With a spatula, transfer the polenta to a bowl and, with a whisk or fork, stir in the butter. Divide the polenta among 4 bowls. Top with the ragù and finish with a sprinkle of Parmigiano Reggiano cheese.

## Getting Juiced for Stock

Fresh vegetable juices make incredible cooking liquids—and are often much purer and tastier than purchased vegetable broth. You can even combine a few items (like carrot-beet-ginger), blend in some fresh herbs (basil, cilantro), and you have a wonderfully flavorful cooking liquid to plump rice, cook polenta, or make a soup. You can get fresh juice from the grocery store—there is often pure bottled carrot juice in the produce area. Or get it freshly juiced at a local juice bar or smoothie shop. They can even juice in some herbs and other stuff for you—parsley, cilantro, basil, lemon, ginger . . . the more flavor, the better.

# GREEN RICE WITH CHARRED BROCCOLI

(V) (GF) *SERVES 4*

On its own, white rice doesn't provide very much in the way of protein or nutrition, but when you bulk it up with vegetables and herbs, plain white rice becomes supercharged. Here, I turn broccoli florets out onto a preheated sheet pan so they start to singe and caramelize the second they hit the hot surface. I set aside the broccoli while oven-steaming the white rice in an herb broth, which is made by blending lots of herbs with garlic and water—it's a spot-on technique to add richness and depth to rice if you don't have vegetable broth in the house. (Or use vegetable juice in place of water for the herb broth to add an extra flavor kick; see page 112 for ideas.)

This rice works as a side to just about anything, or top it with some crisp tofu or white beans to make a complete meal. Plus, the leftovers are superb stuffed into a burrito or turned into fried rice. And, of course, cauliflower can be used in addition to, or instead of, the broccoli!

---

1½ pounds broccoli florets, chopped into bite-size pieces
3 tablespoons extra-virgin olive oil
1½ teaspoons kosher salt, plus extra as needed

1 cup fresh herb leaves (any combination of basil, chervil, cilantro, dill, fennel fronds, mint, parsley)
2 garlic cloves, roughly chopped
1½ cups long-grain white rice

---

1. Adjust an oven rack to the middle position, place a rimmed sheet pan on top, and preheat the oven to 425°F.

2. Toss the broccoli with 2 tablespoons olive oil and 1 teaspoon salt in a large bowl. Turn the broccoli out onto the heated sheet pan and roast, stirring midway through cooking, until tender and charred in spots, 15 to 20 minutes. Scrape the broccoli back

into the bowl and set it aside. (No need to wash the pan—the browned bits will add flavor to the rice.)

3. While the broccoli cooks, make the herb broth: Combine the herbs, remaining tablespoon olive oil, garlic, remaining ½ teaspoon salt, and 2½ cups water in a blender. Blend at high speed until fully combined.

4. Add the rice to the sheet pan and spread it evenly. Pull the oven rack out partway, place the sheet pan on it and, with a fork, stir in the herb broth. Wearing oven mitts if the pan is still hot, carefully cover the sheet pan with aluminum foil (you may need 2 sheets), crimping it tightly around the edges to seal. Bake until the rice is cooked through, about 25 minutes.

5. Remove the sheet pan from the oven and set it aside, covered, for 10 minutes. Discard the foil and transfer the cooked rice to the bowl with the reserved broccoli. Stir to combine, taste, add more salt if necessary, and serve.

## Sheet Pan Grain Chart

Cooking grains on a sheet pan is a total revelation. It's such a simple and forgiving method. All you really need is a rimmed sheet pan and some foil to create a tight-fitting "lid." (Crimp those edges the best you can!) As a general rule, when I cook grains on a sheet pan, I like to toss them with a teaspoon or two of oil before placing them on the pan. It helps keep the grains separate and not clumped together. And if I'm adding the grains to a sheet pan that was previously used to roast some veggies, I don't bother cleaning it first. All that stuff on the pan? Extra flavor!

Following are ratios for grain to liquid— water, herb water, or broth—as well as cooking times for each. Experiment a bit and have some fun.

| GRAIN (4 SERVINGS) | BOILING LIQUID | TEMPERATURE & TIME |
| --- | --- | --- |
| Black rice (forbidden rice): 1½ cups | 3 cups | 350°F, 35 to 40 minutes |
| Bulgur: 1½ cups | 3 cups | 350°F, 10 minutes; rest 10 minutes, covered |
| Couscous*: 1½ cups | 2¼ cups | 350°F, 12 minutes; rest 5 minutes, covered |
| Long-grain brown rice: 1½ cups | 3 cups | 350°F, 35 to 40 minutes |
| Long-grain white rice: 1½ cups | 2 cups | 350°F, 25 minutes |
| Short-grain white rice: 2 cups | 3 cups | 350°F, 20 minutes |
| Quinoa*: 1½ cups, rinsed well | 2 cups | 350°F, 20 minutes, stir midway through cooking |

*Technically not a grain, but it cooks beautifully on a sheet pan!

# Chapter 5

# BEANS AND LEGUMES

Beans and legumes are the holy grail of protein and B vitamins for a vegetable-forward diet. Low in fat and insanely healthy, they also fill your belly for hours to come, offering bonus feelings of contentment and satiated joy. In this chapter you'll find some bean-y classics, like chili and super-delicious baked beans. I've also included lots of lentils, which are very inexpensive and loaded with vitamins and minerals, plus they can be cooked from scratch on a sheet pan. (Dried beans don't fare so well on a sheet pan, so I always use canned.) You'll find the pulses tucked into delicate squash halves (page 116), confetti-sprinkled into rice with crispy shallots (page 133), and turned into Indian spice-scented daal (page 135)—one of my favorite comforting meals in a bowl. Beans are also excellent for blitzing into meatballs (page 128) and burgers (page 123) and a beet loaf (page 138). (Get it? Like meatloaf but . . . beets!)

# LENTIL- AND SPINACH-STUFFED SQUASH HALVES

(V) (GF) *SERVES 4*

Hearty and gorgeous, this is a wonderful dinner party dish or even a centerpiece for the Thanksgiving table. You can swap hollowed zucchini halves or bell pepper halves for the Delicata squash, or make a really colorful platter by stuffing and roasting all three. If lentils aren't your jam, you can use any kind of bean instead—from giant white gigantes to little navy beans.

---

2 delicata winter squash (about 1 pound each), halved lengthwise and seeded
3 tablespoons extra-virgin olive oil
3 teaspoons kosher salt, plus extra as needed
1 teaspoon freshly ground black pepper
8 ounces brown mushrooms, stemmed and thinly sliced
1 medium-size red onion, finely chopped
2 teaspoons cumin seeds
1 teaspoon dried oregano
1 teaspoon ground coriander

1 teaspoon garlic powder
1 teaspoon sweet paprika
½ teaspoon dried thyme
1 cup boiling water
1 can (15 ounces) lentils, drained and rinsed
8 cups lightly packed fresh spinach, roughly chopped
1 lemon, halved, one half cut into 4 wedges
Wedge of Parmigiano Reggiano cheese, shaved with a vegetable peeler into ribbons, for serving (optional)

---

1. Adjust an oven rack to the middle position and preheat the oven to 400°F.

2. Cut a very thin slice off the rounded skin side of each squash half so they rest like a canoe. Rub 1 tablespoon olive oil over the squash halves, inside and out, and season evenly with 1 teaspoon salt and ½ teaspoon pepper. Place the squash halves, cut side up on a rimmed baking sheet and roast until a paring knife slips easily into the center of the squash, 50 to 60 minutes. Transfer the squash to a large platter and set it aside.

# SHEET PAN CHILI

**VO** **GF** *SERVES 4*

A sheet pan is a great vehicle for making a reasonable amount of chili (like when you're not hosting a roomful of hungry Super Bowl watchers). This one comes together in about an hour and has all the classic chili flavors—peppers, garlic, chili, and cumin—plus lots of tomatoes and beans, of course. I like adding veggie crumbles, too, for that hearty chili texture. You can find veggie crumbles in the freezer aisle where the veggie burgers are, or substitute crumbled tempeh instead. This is so good served with Fresh Corn Cornbread (page 159) on the side. I like tossing leftovers with elbow pasta, grated cheese, and scallions for chili mac (or spoon it over the mac and cheese on page 144).

---

1 red onion, finely chopped

2 tablespoons extra-virgin olive oil

1 teaspoon kosher salt

½ teaspoon freshly ground black pepper

2 medium-size red bell peppers, stemmed and seeded, 1 finely chopped, the other cut into ¾-inch pieces

2 medium-size green bell peppers, stemmed and seeded, 1 finely chopped, the other cut into ¾-inch pieces

2 garlic cloves, minced

1 tablespoon chili powder

1 teaspoon ground cumin

1 teaspoon dried oregano

¼ teaspoon cayenne

3¼ cups (about 26 ounces) canned chopped tomatoes

3 cups (about 11 ounces) veggie crumbles (optional)

1 can (15 ounces) black beans or pinto beans, drained and rinsed

½ pound green beans, ends trimmed, beans halved on a sharp diagonal

¼ cup finely chopped fresh cilantro leaves

Chopped avocado, shredded Cheddar cheese, thinly sliced scallions, finely chopped jalapeño chiles, sour cream, and/or tortilla chips, for serving (optional)

---

1. Adjust an oven rack to the middle position and preheat the oven to 375°F.

2. Toss the red onion with the olive oil, ½ teaspoon salt, and the pepper on a rimmed sheet pan. Roast until the onion is soft and just starting to brown, about 15 minutes.

3. Add the finely chopped red and green bell peppers (save the ¾-inch pieces for Step 4), the garlic, chili powder, cumin, oregano, and

cayenne. Cook and stir to combine until the peppers are soft, about 15 minutes more.

4. Remove the sheet pan from the oven and add the tomatoes, veggie crumbles (if using), black beans, green beans, ¾-inch bell pepper pieces, 1 cup water, and the remaining ½ teaspoon salt. Stir gently to combine. Wearing oven mitts, carefully cover the sheet pan with aluminum foil (you may need 2 sheets), crimping it loosely around the edges to seal. Return the sheet pan to the oven and continue to bake, stirring midway through cooking, until the water reduces and the flavors come together, about 30 minutes. Divide among bowls, sprinkle with cilantro, and serve with the toppings of your choice.

# BLACK BEAN AND QUINOA VEGGIE BURGERS

V *MAKES 6 BURGERS*

Crispy on the outside and tender within, these veggie burgers hit all the right spots. You cook the vegetables and quinoa on a sheet pan first, then blitz in the seasonings, beans, and panko bread crumbs in a food processor or blender. These are also great for making ahead: You can freeze the patties on a sheet pan until semifrozen, wrap each individually in aluminum foil, and freeze in a resealable freezer bag. To cook, simply place the foil-wrapped burger in a 350°F oven until warmed through, about 20 minutes, then brown it on a sheet pan according to the instructions in Step 6 or in a hot, greased skillet.

¼ cup extra-virgin olive oil
1 medium-size portobello mushroom, finely chopped
1 medium-size red or yellow onion, stemmed, seeded, and finely chopped
1 medium-size red or orange bell pepper, stemmed, seeded, and finely chopped
1 medium-size carrot, finely chopped
½ medium-size sweet potato, peeled and finely chopped
2 teaspoons kosher salt
½ teaspoon freshly ground black pepper
1¾ cups boiling water
¾ cup quinoa, rinsed

1 can (15 ounces) black beans, drained and rinsed
⅔ cup panko bread crumbs
2 tablespoons nutritional yeast
1 tablespoon finely chopped fresh rosemary leaves
1 teaspoon garlic powder
Cheese slices of choice, for serving (optional)
6 hamburger buns, toasted or untoasted
Lettuce, tomato slices, onion slices, pickles, avocado slices, mustard, ketchup, hot sauce, and/or other toppings of your choice, for serving (optional)

1. Adjust an oven rack to the middle position, place a rimmed sheet pan on it, and preheat the oven to 425°F.

2. Toss together 2 tablespoons olive oil, the mushroom, onion, bell pepper, carrot, sweet potato, 1 teaspoon salt, and the pepper in a large bowl.

Transfer the vegetables to the heated sheet pan and roast, stirring once, until they start to brown, about 15 minutes. Reduce the oven temperature to 350°F.

3. Wearing oven mitts, pull the oven rack out partway and carefully add the boiling water to the pan followed by the quinoa, stirring to submerge it as best you can. Cover the pan with aluminum foil (you may need 2 sheets), crimping it around the edges to seal. Cook until the quinoa is fluffy and cooked through and the vegetables are tender, 25 to 30 minutes. Remove the pan from the oven (turn off the oven) and let sit, covered, for 10 minutes. Uncover and cool slightly.

4. Transfer the quinoa mixture to the bowl of a food processor. Add the black beans, bread crumbs, nutritional yeast, rosemary, garlic powder, and remaining teaspoon salt and pulse until the mixture is semi-rough yet holds together when squeezed, about eight (1-second) pulses. Transfer the mixture to a medium-size bowl. Wash and dry the sheet pan.

5. Return the cleaned sheet pan to the oven rack and increase the oven temperature to 400°F. Lay a sheet of plastic wrap on your work surface and, with a ½-cup measure, scoop out 6 mounds of the mixture. Gently press each mound into a ½-inch-thick patty, about 3½ inches wide.

6. Add the remaining 2 tablespoons olive oil to the heated pan and let it warm in the oven for 2 minutes. Place the patties on the pan (discard the plastic wrap), and bake until the patties are browned on the bottom, about 10 minutes. Turn them and cook on the other side, about 10 minutes more. Top the burgers with cheese (if using) and return them to the oven until the cheese melts. Otherwise, serve the burgers on a bun with toppings of your choice.

# WHITE BEAN RATATOUILLE OVER ROASTED EGGPLANT

(V) (GF)  SERVES 6

**I** wait for it all year long—that moment at the green market when
*everything* seems to be in season and gorgeous—eggplants, tomatoes,
peppers, herbs, summer squash. . . . There seems to be no end to the
glorious bounty of pitch-perfect produce. Ratatouille is a complete
celebration of this finery. On a sheet pan, the hot, yet even, oven heat
coaxes out the sweetness of the vegetables without turning them to mush.
Instead of adding eggplant to the ratatouille, I roast it separately in big,
thick slices, then spoon the tomato-bean mixture right over the top to
dress up this quite rustic dish. If you prefer, chop the eggplant into small
pieces and roast it along with the onion in Step 3.

---

1 large eggplant (about 1½ pounds),
   stem and base removed, and
   sliced crosswise into 6 (1-inch)
   thick rounds
6 tablespoons extra-virgin olive oil
2 garlic cloves, minced
1¾ teaspoons kosher salt
1 medium-size red onion, finely
   chopped
1 medium-size red bell pepper,
   stemmed, seeded, and finely
   chopped

2 medium-size zucchini, chopped
   into bite-size pieces
¼ teaspoon crushed red pepper
   flakes (optional)
1 large tomato (about 1 pound),
   chopped (about 2 cups)
1 can (15 ounces) cannellini beans,
   drained and rinsed
½ cup fresh basil leaves, stacked,
   rolled, and thinly sliced crosswise
   into ribbons

---

1. Adjust an oven rack to the middle
   position and preheat the oven to
   375°F.

2. Place the eggplant slices on a
   rimmed sheet pan. Mix 3 tablespoons
   olive oil, the garlic, and ½ teaspoon

salt together in a small bowl. Brush
both sides of each eggplant slice
with the garlic oil mixture (save any
leftover garlic oil for the tomatoes).
Roast the eggplant until the bottoms
are browned, about 15 minutes.
With a spatula, flip the slices and

continue to roast until tender, about 10 minutes more. Transfer the eggplant to a large plate.

3. Add the red onion and 2 tablespoons olive oil to the sheet pan, sprinkle with ¾ teaspoon salt, and stir to coat. Roast until the onion becomes translucent and starts to brown around the edges, about 10 minutes. Stir in the red bell pepper and cook until it starts to soften, about 10 minutes. Add the zucchini, crushed red pepper flakes (if using), and remaining tablespoon olive oil and continue to cook until the onions are browned and the zucchini starts to become tender, about 10 minutes more.

4. Mix the tomatoes, remaining garlic oil, and remaining ½ teaspoon salt in a medium-size bowl. With a spatula, push the vegetable mixture to the one side of the sheet pan; turn the tomatoes out onto the other side. Roast until the tomatoes start to look juicy, about 10 minutes. Add the beans to the tomatoes and cook just enough to warm them through, 5 minutes more. Remove the sheet pan from the oven and transfer the vegetables and beans to a large bowl. Add most of the basil and stir to combine.

5. Place 1 eggplant slice on each of 6 plates. Top with a generous amount of the bean mixture, sprinkle with the remaining basil, and serve.

# EGGPLANT AND WHITE BEAN MEATBALLS

**GF** *MAKES 22 MEATBALLS*

Tender and hearty, these meatballs are so good that most meatball lovers will hardly miss the meat, especially when they're tossed with marinara, cheese, and spaghetti. To make the meatballs gluten free, use gluten-free bread crumbs. I love using leftovers on the Meatball, Pepper, and Onion Grinders (page 131).

---

1 large eggplant (about 1¼ pounds)
1 large egg
⅔ cup cooked cannellini beans (canned are fine)
2 garlic cloves, minced
½ cup packed fresh basil leaves
½ cup finely grated Pecorino Romano or Parmigiano Reggiano cheese, plus extra for serving
1 teaspoon kosher salt

½ teaspoon freshly ground black pepper
¼ teaspoon crushed red pepper flakes
1½ cups panko bread crumbs or gluten-free bread crumbs
2 tablespoons extra-virgin olive oil
3 cups (24-ounce jar) favorite store-bought marinara sauce, warmed

---

1. Adjust an oven rack to the middle position and preheat the oven to 375°F. Line a rimmed sheet pan with aluminum foil.

2. Prick the eggplant 4 times with a fork and place it on the prepared sheet pan. Roast the eggplant until it completely collapses and a paring knife inserted into the center meets no resistance, about 1 hour. Remove the eggplant from the oven (turn off the oven) and cut an X into its base. Stand the eggplant upright in a fine-mesh sieve or colander placed in the sink so the juices can drain and the eggplant can cool, about 20 minutes.

3. Place the eggplant on a cutting board and, with a chef's knife, make a slit lengthwise from end to end to open it up. Scoop out the flesh and add it to the bowl of a food processor. Add the egg, beans, garlic, basil, cheese, salt, pepper, and crushed red pepper flakes. Process for five or six (1-second) pulses, add the bread crumbs, and pulse two more times to combine.

4. Place a rimmed sheet pan on the oven rack, and heat the oven to 400°F. Shape the eggplant mixture into 22 balls, each the size of a small plum. Add the olive oil to the heated sheet pan and return it to the oven to warm for 2 minutes. Carefully place the meatballs on the pan (it will be hot—take care not to burn yourself), spacing them evenly, and roast until they are browned on the bottom, about 10 minutes. With a spatula, turn the meatballs and roast until the other sides are browned, 10 minutes more. Serve with the marinara and extra cheese.

# MEATBALL, PEPPER, AND ONION GRINDERS

*MAKES 4 SANDWICHES*

**M**aking a great sandwich is truly an art. There has to be a balance of fresh and cooked, warm and cold, crunchy and tender—and, in a perfect world, you get all these flavors and textures in each and every bite. Here, I top Eggplant and White Bean Meatballs (page 128) with fresh basil; snappy and piquant pickled cherry peppers; caramelized onions and bell peppers; and melted, stringy provolone cheese. Is it art? Perhaps. Either way, it sure is good.

---

1 red onion, halved and thinly sliced
1 green bell pepper, stemmed, seeded, and thinly sliced
¼ cup extra-virgin olive oil
¾ teaspoon kosher salt
½ teaspoon freshly ground black pepper
4 sub rolls, halved lengthwise
12 to 16 warm Eggplant and White Bean Meatballs (page 128) or any homemade vegetarian meatballs

¾ cup favorite marinara sauce
¼ cup fresh basil leaves, stacked, rolled, and thinly sliced crosswise into ribbons
8 slices provolone cheese
¼ cup chopped pickled hot peppers, such as cherry peppers or giardiniera (optional)

---

1. Adjust an oven rack to the upper-middle position, place a rimmed sheet pan on top, and preheat the oven to 425°F.

2. Toss the red onion and bell pepper with 2 tablespoons olive oil, the salt, and pepper in a large bowl and turn them out in an even layer onto the heated sheet pan. Roast, stirring after 8 minutes, until the onion and pepper begin to char around the edges, 15 to 18 minutes total. Remove the pan from the oven and transfer the onion and pepper to a bowl (don't wash the sheet pan—you will use it in Step 3).

3. Turn the broiler to high. Line the sheet pan with aluminum foil and place the sub rolls on top, cut side up. Brush the cut sides with the remaining 2 tablespoons olive oil and toast them under the broiler until golden brown, 2 to 3 minutes (watch the bread closely as broiler intensities vary).

4. Remove the top halves from the sheet pan and arrange 3 or 4 meatballs over each bottom half. Lay some onions and peppers over the meatballs, dollop each sub half with 3 tablespoons marinara, sprinkle with basil, and cover each with 2 pieces of provolone cheese. Return the sheet pan to the oven and broil until the cheese melts, about 2 minutes. Place the pickled peppers (if using) on top of the melted cheese, put the sandwiches together, and serve.

# CRISPY ROASTED SHALLOT AND LENTIL MUJADARA

V GF  *SERVES 4*

This is the rice and beans of the Middle East. The trick to developing depth of flavor is to get the shallots nicely browned—actually nearly (but not quite) crispy-burnt so they flavor the lentils with their caramelized rich oniony flavor. Starting the lentils first ensures they'll cook through and become tender once the rice has absorbed all the liquid and is nice and fluffy. I like to pack this in a container instead of a sandwich for my kids' lunch—the high protein fix is great for days when you need a little extra energy.

---

8 medium-size shallots, halved and
   very thinly sliced
2 tablespoons extra-virgin olive oil
1 tablespoon ground cumin
2 teaspoons dried thyme or
   1 heaping tablespoon finely
   chopped fresh thyme leaves
2½ teaspoons kosher salt, plus extra
   as needed

1 teaspoon freshly ground black
   pepper
¾ cup brown lentils, picked over
   and rinsed
4 cups boiling water
1½ cups long-grain white rice
¼ cup finely chopped fresh flat-leaf
   parsley leaves or cilantro leaves

---

1. Adjust an oven rack to the middle position, place a rimmed sheet pan on top, and preheat the oven to 375°F.

2. Toss the shallots with the olive oil, cumin, thyme, 1 teaspoon salt, and the pepper in a large bowl. Turn the shallots out onto the heated sheet pan in an even layer and cook until they brown, about 25 minutes.

3. Wearing oven mitts, pull the oven rack out partway and stir the lentils into the shallot mixture on the sheet pan. Carefully add the boiling water and cover the sheet pan with aluminum foil (you may need 2 sheets), crimping it around the edges to seal. Reduce the oven temperature to 350°F and bake for 10 minutes.

4. Pull the rack out partway again, open the foil and stir in the rice and remaining 1½ teaspoons salt. Re-cover the sheet pan, crimping the foil around the edges to seal, and continue to cook until the rice is tender, about 25 minutes more.

5. Remove the pan from the oven. Taste and adjust the salt if needed. Sprinkle with the parsley and serve warm or at room temperature.

## Eat. More. Lentils.

Lentils can save the world. Not only are they extra cheap at the grocery store, but they are supremely healthy—loaded with fiber, protein, and folic acid. *Plus* they actually give back to the soil, returning valuable nitrogen from the air back to the ground, thereby creating their own fertilizer without consuming tons of water to grow. I ask you—what is *not* to love?

# INDIAN LENTILS (DAAL)

(V) (GF) *SERVES 4*

D aal is like the chicken soup of India. Look for bright orange *masoor daal* lentils, which cook down to a soft, pulpy consistency. Pair the daal with rice as they do in India for a complete protein that contains all your necessary amino acids—and did you know 1 cup of cooked lentils has 17 grams of protein? Talk about bang for your buck!

3 tablespoons neutral vegetable oil (such as grapeseed or safflower)
1 medium-size red onion, finely chopped
1 serrano or jalapeño chile, stemmed (seeded for reduced heat, if you like) and finely chopped
3 garlic cloves, finely minced
3 dried red chiles or ½ teaspoon crushed red pepper flakes
1 tablespoon grated fresh ginger
2 teaspoons cumin seeds

1 teaspoon ground coriander
1 teaspoon brown mustard seeds
1 tomato, cored and finely chopped
1 teaspoon ground turmeric
1 cup orange lentils (*masoor daal*)
3 cups boiling water
1½ teaspoons kosher salt, plus extra as needed
½ cup roughly chopped fresh cilantro leaves, for garnish
Sheet pan rice (page 114) or steamed rice, for serving (optional)

1. Adjust an oven rack to the middle position, place a sheet pan on top, and preheat the oven to 350°F.

2. Combine the vegetable oil, red onion, serrano, garlic, dried red chiles, ginger, cumin seeds, coriander, and mustard seeds in a small bowl. Pour this mix onto the heated sheet pan and bake, stirring midway through cooking, until the onion starts to brown, 12 to 15 minutes.

3. Stir in the tomato and turmeric and return the sheet pan to the oven for 10 minutes. Wearing oven mitts, carefully pull the oven rack out partway and add the lentils and boiling water to the sheet pan. Cover the sheet pan with aluminum foil (you may need 2 sheets), crimping it around the edges to seal. Cook until the lentils are tender, about 25 minutes.

4. Remove the pan from the oven and stir in the salt. Taste and add more salt if needed. Sprinkle with cilantro and serve with rice on the side (if using).

# BARBECUE BAKED BEANS WITH MUSHROOM "LARDONS"

(V) (GF) *SERVES 4*

**S**weet and hearty, baked beans over toast is a winter favorite. They're also great as a side with Hoisin-Glazed Beet Loaf (page 138), or with rice or quinoa for a complete protein. The mushrooms here are roasted until they are very tight, browned, and almost chewy. They add a bacon-y quality to the beans—for a little extra smokiness, finish with a pinch of smoked flaky salt. These beans are also a winner sprinkled onto a salad or a pizza.

### FOR THE BEANS
¼ cup light brown sugar
¼ cup dark molasses
¼ cup tomato paste
1 teaspoon kosher salt
½ teaspoon ground cinnamon
½ teaspoon dry mustard
½ teaspoon freshly grated nutmeg
½ teaspoon freshly ground black
   pepper
1 small yellow onion, finely chopped
1 jalapeño chile, stemmed
   (seeded for reduced heat,
   if you like) and finely chopped

2 tablespoons neutral vegetable oil
   (such as grapeseed or safflower)
2 cans (15 ounces each) pinto beans,
   drained and rinsed

### FOR THE MUSHROOM LARDONS
8 ounces portobello or shiitake
   mushrooms, stemmed and caps
   cut into ½-inch cubes
3 tablespoons neutral vegetable oil
   (such as grapeseed or safflower)
½ teaspoon smoked flaky salt
   (or kosher salt)

1. To make the beans: Adjust an oven rack to the middle position, place a rimmed sheet pan on top, and preheat the oven to 400°F.

2. Whisk the brown sugar, molasses, tomato paste, salt, cinnamon, mustard, nutmeg, and pepper in a medium-size bowl.

3. Toss the onion and jalapeño with the vegetable oil in a separate medium-size bowl and turn them out onto the heated sheet pan. Add the brown sugar mixture and beans along with 1¼ cups water. Wearing oven mitts, carefully cover the pan with aluminum foil (you may need 2 sheets), crimping it around the

edges to seal. Bake until the onion and jalapeño are tender, the sauce is warmed through and bubbling, and the flavors have come together, about 35 minutes.

4. Meanwhile, make the mushroom lardons: Combine the mushrooms with the vegetable oil on a second rimmed sheet pan and roast in the oven next to the beans, stirring occasionally, until they are very browned and have released all their moisture, 25 to 35 minutes. Sprinkle with the smoked salt and toss to coat.

5. Divide the beans among 4 bowls and serve with the mushroom lardons sprinkled over the top.

## Baked Beans with . . .

So you just baked up a nice, big sheet pan of beans. Now what? Here are some tasty ways to stretch the protein- and fiber-filled batch throughout the week.

**MONDAY:** Baked beans over toast with a side salad

**TUESDAY:** Baked beans and quinoa bowl (see page 114) with avocado, shredded cheese, and cilantro

**WEDNESDAY:** Baked beans pureed with water, garlic, and rosemary for bean dip

**THURSDAY:** Three-bean salad with baked beans, steamed green beans, and chickpeas

**FRIDAY:** Baked bean and roasted potato hash with a fried egg on top

**SATURDAY/SUNDAY:** Seven-layer bean dip: baked beans, sour cream, cheese, guacamole, salsa, shredded lettuce, chopped tomatoes

# HOISIN-GLAZED BEET LOAF

(VO) *SERVES 4*

**H**old the phone. You don't believe me? You don't think this could actually taste like meatloaf? Well, you know what . . . ? It doesn't—it's *better*. That's right—bold statement, I know, but this loaf is sweet and spicy and moist and tender and all the things you love in a meatloaf—minus the meat! Instead you get so much protein, fiber, vitamins, and minerals from a beet, a giant portobello mushroom, beans, pecans, and flax meal. And the spicy-sweet hoisin glaze brings it all together. Not only is this great as a main course, but the leftovers are UNBEATABLE as a meatloaf sandwich with pickles the next day! With baked beans (page 136) you have a meal fit for a superhero.

---

**FOR THE BEET LOAF**

¾ cup bulgur

1½ cups boiling water

1 large beet (about 8 ounces), peeled

1 large portobello mushroom, stemmed and quartered

1 can (15 ounces) pinto beans, drained and rinsed

⅔ cup pecan pieces

2 tablespoons flax meal (see box, page 139)

1 tablespoon Dijon mustard

1 tablespoon soy sauce

1 teaspoon ground coriander

½ teaspoon Chinese five-spice powder

1½ teaspoons kosher salt

¾ teaspoon freshly ground black pepper

2 tablespoons extra-virgin olive oil

**FOR THE GLAZE**

⅓ cup ketchup

⅓ cup hoisin sauce

1 tablespoon honey or agave syrup

½ teaspoon smoked paprika

⅛ to ¼ teaspoon cayenne pepper (depending on how spicy you want the glaze)

¼ teaspoon kosher salt

---

**1.** Adjust an oven rack to the middle position and preheat the oven to 350°F.

**2.** Spread the bulgur on a rimmed sheet pan, pull the oven rack out partway, and place the sheet pan on it. Carefully add the boiling water and, wearing oven mitts, cover the sheet pan with aluminum foil (you may need 2 sheets), crimping it tightly around the edges to seal. Cook the bulgur for 10 minutes, remove the pan from the oven, and set it aside, covered, for 10 minutes. Remove the foil and fluff the bulgur with a fork.

3. Using a food processor fitted with the grater attachment (or the medium-size holes of a box grater), shred the beet and the mushroom. Swap the grater attachment for the blade and add the beans, pecans, flax meal, mustard, soy sauce, coriander, five-spice powder, salt, and pepper. Add the bulgur (wipe the sheet pan clean; you'll use it in Step 4) and pulse to combine so the mixture is finely ground yet still rough—you don't want a smooth paste.

4. Line the sheet pan with a piece of aluminum foil and lightly coat the foil with olive oil. Transfer the bulgur mixture to the sheet pan and form the mixture into a log, 9 inches long, 4 inches wide, and approximately 1½ inches thick. Bake the beet loaf until it's somewhat firm and browned, about 25 minutes.

5. Meanwhile, make the glaze: Stir together the ketchup, hoisin, honey, paprika, cayenne, and salt in a small bowl. Once the loaf has cooked for 25 minutes, use a pastry brush or silicone brush to coat the surface of the loaf with half the glaze. Return the loaf to the oven and cook for 15 minutes more. Brush the remaining glaze over the loaf and turn the broiler to high. Broil the loaf until the glaze begins to caramelize and brown, 3 to 4 minutes (watch the glaze closely as broiler intensities vary). Remove the sheet pan from the oven and cool for 10 minutes. Use the foil to help transfer the loaf to a cutting board. Slice the loaf crosswise into ½- to ¾-inch-thick pieces and serve.

## Flax Magic

You can use whole flaxseed in seed form or ground into a meal (also called a "flour"). When pulverized and combined with liquid, the flax has a binding effect that holds dough or meals together much like "vegan eggs" (but without the leavening boost), which is how it is used in this beet loaf. Flaxseed is highly nutritious— among all the foods we eat, scientists score flaxseed as the number one source of lignans, a phytonutrient and antioxidant-rich source of polyphenols that can work to help boost the body's response against free radicals that can cause cancer. Flaxseed is also rich in heart-healthy omega-3 fatty acids. While it is often added to egg-free dishes for a binding effect, you can also add a few tablespoons to a recipe in addition to the flours, eggs, and other ingredients to boost your recipes in a nutritionally positive way.

Because it is so rich in fats, flax meal can turn "off tasting" quickly; it's best stored in the freezer to preserve its freshness. Flaxseed can be found in health food stores and, increasingly, in the grocery store aisle where you might find gluten-free flour substitutes and grains and other meals such as almond meal, quinoa, and tapioca flour.

# Chapter 6

# PASTA, BREAD, AND PIZZA

Pizza and focaccia on a sheet pan is a bit of a no-brainer. I mean, of course they're going to work. You can buy refrigerated dough in most supermarkets, or just stop in at your favorite pizzeria and ask them if you can buy a few rounds of dough. Unless it's some highly guarded recipe, they're usually happy to sell it to you for a buck or two a ball. What I think is so cool and interesting here is that you can make PASTA on a sheet pan! Oh, yeah! Couscous is fast and simple, steaming in mere minutes much like bulgur (page 114). I make a No-Boil Mac and Cheese (page 144) in which the pasta cooks right in the sauce (same for the Orzo with Pan-Roasted Tomatoes, Lemon, and Mozzarella, page 147), and use no-boil noodles, which need no pre-cooking, in the Roasted Vegetable Lasagna (page 156). I also include a sheet pan Fresh Corn Cornbread (page 159) that is awesome with the Sheet Pan Chili (page 120), the White Bean Ratatouille over Roasted Eggplant (page 125), or nearly anything saucy and delicious.

# LARGE PEARL COUSCOUS WITH FRESH CORN, ZUCCHINI, AND BASIL

(VO)  *SERVES 4*

**B**rowning butter by melting it and allowing the milk solids to caramelize gives it a hazelnut-like quality that quickly elevates the flavor of just about anything you toss with it (see page 143). Usually it is made by melting and swirling the butter in a saucepan, but making browned butter on a sheet pan actually takes less time as the shallow depth of the pan allows the butter to brown more quickly. Here, it gives a wonderful toasty taste to large pearl couscous, sweet summer corn, zucchini, and basil. The whole dish takes about 30 minutes to prepare from start to finish but you'd never guess it from the complexity of its flavors.

---

4 tablespoons (½ stick) unsalted butter, cut into 4 pieces
3 ears fresh corn, shucked and kernels sliced off the cob
1 large zucchini, chopped into ¼- to ½-inch pieces (about the size of the corn kernels)

1½ teaspoons kosher salt, plus extra as needed
1½ cups large pearl couscous
3 cups boiling water
½ cup fresh basil leaves, stacked, rolled, and thinly sliced crosswise into ribbons

---

**1.** Adjust an oven rack to the middle position and preheat the oven to 350°F.

**2.** Place the butter on a rimmed sheet pan and set it in the oven until the butter melts and smells toasty and nutty, about 4 minutes. Remove the sheet pan from the oven and pour about half of the browned butter into a small heatproof bowl.

**3.** Stir the corn and zucchini into the remaining butter on the sheet pan and cook until the zucchini softens and the corn loses its raw starchiness, 6 to 8 minutes. Transfer the corn mixture to a medium-size bowl and season with ½ teaspoon salt.

4. Add the couscous to the pan along with the boiling water and the remaining 1 teaspoon salt. Stir to combine, and wearing oven mitts, cover the sheet pan with aluminum foil (you may need 2 sheets), crimping it tightly around the edges to seal. Bake for 10 minutes, then remove the foil, stir the couscous, re-cover the pan, and continue to cook until the couscous is plump and tender, about 10 minutes more.

5. Transfer the couscous to a large bowl. Add the reserved butter, most of the basil, and the corn and zucchini mixture. Taste for salt, adding more if needed, and serve sprinkled with the remaining basil.

## More Ways with Browned Butter

Make a double batch of browned butter in Step 2 and use it like this:

- Chill until solid and use as the butter in recipes for cakes and cookies for a nutty and wonderfully rich butter flavor

- Cool and spread on toast

- For frying eggs or potatoes

- Toss with pasta and freshly grated cheese, or drizzle over any roasted or steamed vegetable (steamed cauliflower, blanched green beans, and roasted carrots are a few of my favorite vegetable pairings)

- Add to pancake or waffle batter

- Drizzle into vegetable mashes: potatoes, cauliflower, rutabaga . . .

# NO-BOIL
# MAC AND CHEESE

*SERVES 6 TO 8*

I t's pretty cool that you can make mac and cheese on a sheet pan in the oven—no fuss, no muss, and no pre-boiling pasta necessary! It's ultra creamy thanks to evaporated milk, a good bit of heavy cream (you could substitute half-and-half, if you like), and not a shy amount of cheese! For extra nutrition (and less fat) try substituting 1 cup vegetable puree for 1 cup cream. It will be less dairy rich but still creamy and luscious—carrots, cauliflower, and butternut squash all work well. (You can even use jarred baby food in a pinch.)

2 tablespoons unsalted butter at room temperature, plus 2 tablespoons melted

2 cups dry, plain bread crumbs (I like Japanese panko)

1 cup finely grated Parmigiano Reggiano cheese (preferably freshly grated)

1½ cups whole milk

1 can (15 ounces) evaporated milk

1½ cups heavy (whipping) cream

2 tablespoons dehydrated onion

1 teaspoon garlic powder

1 teaspoon kosher salt

8 ounces (about 2 cups) freshly shredded sharp Cheddar cheese (preferably orange cheese)

8 ounces (about 2 cups) freshly shredded fontina cheese

1 box (16 ounces) elbow macaroni, uncooked

1. Adjust an oven rack to the middle position and preheat the oven to 375°F.

2. Grease a rimmed sheet pan with the room-temperature butter and set aside. Combine the bread crumbs and Parmigiano Reggiano cheese in a medium-size bowl. Stir in the melted butter and set aside.

3. Whisk the whole milk, evaporated milk, cream, onion, garlic powder, salt, and the Cheddar and fontina cheeses in a large bowl. Add the uncooked macaroni and stir until well coated. Pour the mixture into the prepared sheet pan, spreading it in an even layer. Cover the sheet pan with aluminum foil (you may need 2 sheets), crimping it tightly around the edges to seal (make sure to get a good seal on the foil, otherwise the pasta won't cook). Bake for 25 minutes.

4. Wearing oven mitts, remove the foil and stir the macaroni. Sprinkle the bread crumb mixture over the top and continue to bake for 25 minutes more.

5. Turn the broiler to high and broil the macaroni and cheese until it is golden brown on top and bubbling, about 10 minutes (watch the macaroni and cheese closely as broiler intensities vary). Remove from the oven and let the pasta stand, covered, 5 minutes before serving.

# ORZO WITH PAN-ROASTED TOMATOES, LEMON, AND MOZZARELLA

VO  SERVES 4

**N**o. Boil. Pasta. That's right! Small pasta such as orzo works beautifully in a sheet pan. Because of the starches in the pasta (usually you lose some of them when you drain the pasta water), it becomes wonderfully creamy and comforting. Along with the tomatoes, I roast lemons in the sheet pan—the resulting flavor is softly acidic and warm, incredible intertwined with the soft herbaceousness of the vermouth. Meyer lemons have a beautiful sweet lemon flavor and are nice if you can find them in season (usually late fall through winter). Leave out the cheese for a vegan version.

---

1 pound cherry tomatoes, halved
1 medium-size lemon, thinly sliced
   into rounds, seeds removed
3 garlic cloves, very thinly sliced
2 teaspoons kosher salt
½ teaspoon freshly ground black
   pepper
¼ teaspoon crushed red pepper
   flakes
⅓ cup extra-virgin olive oil
⅓ cup dry vermouth or
   dry white wine

1 box (16 ounces) orzo pasta
3¾ cups boiling water
¼ cup fresh basil leaves, stacked,
   rolled, and thinly sliced crosswise
   into ribbons
6 ounces fresh mozzarella cheese,
   roughly torn by hand
¼ cup finely grated Parmigiano
   Reggiano cheese
   (preferably freshly grated)

---

**1.** Adjust an oven rack to the middle position, place a sheet pan on the rack, and preheat the oven to 400°F.

**2.** Place the tomatoes, lemon, garlic, 1 teaspoon salt, pepper, crushed red pepper flakes, and the olive oil in a medium-size bowl and toss to combine. Carefully turn the tomato mixture out onto the heated sheet pan, spread it in an even layer, and roast for 10 minutes.

3. Remove the sheet pan from the oven and stir the vermouth into the tomato mixture. With a silicone spatula, press down on the tomatoes and lemon slices to extract their juices. Stir in the orzo.

4. Pull the oven rack out partway and set the sheet pan on it. Carefully pour the boiling water into the orzo, stirring to combine and distribute evenly. Wearing oven mitts, cover the sheet pan with aluminum foil (you may need 2 sheets), crimping it tightly around the edges to seal. Bake the pasta for 15 minutes.

5. Uncover the pan, add the remaining 1 teaspoon salt, stir the orzo, and cook, uncovered, to allow the juices to thicken and any partially cooked pasta from the top layer to absorb more liquid, 5 minutes more.

6. Preheat the broiler to high. Stir most of the basil into the pasta, then scatter the mozzarella cheese over the top. Sprinkle the Parmigiano Reggiano cheese over the mozzarella and broil until the cheese is melted and golden, 3 to 5 minutes (watch the cheese closely as broiler intensities vary). Remove from the oven and let stand for a few minutes. Sprinkle the remaining basil over the top just before serving.

# BOK CHOY AND PORTOBELLOS OVER RICE VERMICELLI

(V) (GF) SERVES 4

I'm always searching for hearty and healthy meals to pack as a school lunch for my kids. This pasta dish can sit out for hours without losing its deliciousness or raising any temperature-sensitive-ingredient red flags. Rice vermicelli noodles are a great thing to have in the pantry—just add boiling water and soak them for a few minutes for a nice, light meal on the fly.

---

1 pound portobello mushroom caps
2 tablespoons neutral vegetable oil (such as grapeseed or safflower)
¾ teaspoon kosher salt
3 tablespoons hoisin sauce
1 head bok choy or 2 heads baby bok choy (about 1 pound total)
1 package (8 ounces) rice vermicelli noodles
¼ cup soy sauce

2 tablespoons mirin (rice wine)
2 teaspoons toasted sesame oil
1½ teaspoons Sriracha
2 garlic cloves, finely minced
1½ teaspoons freshly grated ginger
4 scallions, trimmed, white and light green parts separated, both thinly sliced on a diagonal
¼ cup chopped fresh cilantro leaves

---

1. Adjust an oven rack to the middle position and preheat the oven to 400°F.

2. Line a rimmed sheet pan with aluminum foil. Rub the mushroom caps all over with 1 tablespoon vegetable oil and place them, stem-side up, on the sheet pan. Sprinkle with ½ teaspoon salt and roast until they just become tender, about 10 minutes. Turn the mushroom caps and brush the tops with 2 tablespoons hoisin sauce. Return the mushrooms to the oven and roast until the tops look dry, about 5 minutes. Transfer the mushrooms to a cutting board and set aside to cool. Slice them into thin strips (save the sheet pan to roast the bok choy).

3. Meanwhile, cut off and discard the bok choy's tough base and separate the white stalks from the leafy tops. Slice the stalks on a diagonal into ½-inch-thick pieces. Stack the leaves, roll them into a cylinder, and thinly slice them crosswise into ribbons. Place the stalks in a medium-size bowl and toss with the remaining tablespoon vegetable oil and the remaining ¼ teaspoon salt. Turn them out onto the sheet pan used for the mushrooms and roast until tender, 8 to 10 minutes. Stir in the leaves and roast for 2 minutes more.

4. While the bok choy cooks, soak the vermicelli: Place the noodles in a large bowl and follow the package instructions for soaking. Drain the noodles and return them to the bowl.

5. Whisk the soy sauce, mirin, sesame oil, Sriracha, garlic, ginger, and scallion whites in a medium-size bowl. Add the noodles, bok choy, and cilantro and toss to combine. Divide among 4 bowls, divide the mushrooms over the top, sprinkle with the scallion greens, and serve.

# TUSCAN KALE AND WHITE BEAN RIBOLLITA

VO SERVES 4

**K**ale-obsessed Brooklyn has nothing on Tuscany—Tuscans have been eating kale for centuries, going back to the time of the Etruscans when this bean and stale bread soup/stew/casserole was a mainstay. Called ribollita, it is hearty and heartwarming and so incredibly good. I also really love it pureed into a porridge and served warm, topped with lots of olive oil and grated Parmigiano Reggiano cheese. This is the very definition of OG comfort food.

---

3 large shallots, finely chopped

3 medium-size carrots, finely chopped

1 celery stalk, finely chopped

1 red bell pepper, stemmed, seeded, and finely chopped

2 teaspoons kosher salt

¼ teaspoon freshly ground black pepper, plus extra for serving

6 tablespoons extra-virgin olive oil, plus extra for serving

1 medium-size zucchini, finely chopped

3 garlic cloves, thinly sliced

2 teaspoons finely chopped fresh rosemary leaves

1 can (28 ounces) chopped tomatoes with juices

1 can (15 ounces) cannellini beans, drained and rinsed

3 cups vegetable broth

6 cups Tuscan kale (lacinato kale), tough stems removed and leaves roughly chopped

6 cups roughly torn rustic bread

Parmigiano Reggiano cheese, for serving (optional)

---

1. Adjust an oven rack to the middle position and preheat the oven to 375°F.

2. Place the shallots, carrots, celery, bell pepper, 1 teaspoon salt, pepper, and 4 tablespoons olive oil in a large bowl and toss to combine. Turn the mixture out onto a rimmed sheet pan (reserve the bowl for Step 5) and roast until the shallots lose their raw look and the carrots start to become tender, about 10 minutes.

3. Stir in the zucchini, garlic, and rosemary and roast until the zucchini starts to become tender, about 10 minutes more. Stir in the tomatoes, beans, and 2 cups vegetable broth. Wearing oven mitts, cover the sheet pan loosely with aluminum foil and cook for 15 minutes.

4. Carefully uncover the pan. Stir in the kale and ½ teaspoon salt. Add another cup of broth if the pan looks dry, re-cover the pan, and cook until the kale is wilted, about 10 minutes.

5. Add the bread to the large bowl and drizzle with the remaining 2 tablespoons olive oil and ½ teaspoon salt. Toss to combine, then scatter the bread over the ribollita. Turn the broiler to high and broil until the bread turns golden brown, 2 to 4 minutes (watch the bread closely as broiler intensities vary).

6. Divide the ribolitta among 4 bowls. Serve with extra olive oil, pepper, and fresh shavings of Parmigiano Reggiano cheese (if using). Or let the ribollita cool and serve at room temperature.

# ROASTED VEGETABLE LASAGNA

*SERVES 6*

There is, perhaps, no single phrase that makes my kids' eyes light up more than the one that goes like this: "We're having lasagna for dinner" (well, maybe when I say we're having nachos for dinner . . . see page 5). Since this version is based on no-boil noodles, it eliminates the extra step of boiling water and dealing with floppy, easy-to-tear pasta. If you hit the salad bar at the grocery store instead of roasting your own vegetables (great trick!), you can get this sheet pan supper in the oven in mere *minutes*. Double the recipe for a half sheet pan if you're feeding a crowd (or want ample leftovers).

---

1 medium-size zucchini, chopped into ½-inch pieces (about 2 cups)

1 medium-size yellow onion, finely chopped

½ pound eggplant, chopped into ½-inch pieces (about 2 cups)

2 tablespoons extra-virgin olive oil

1 teaspoon kosher salt

3 cups tomato sauce, homemade (page 169) or store-bought

1 box (9 ounces) oven-ready (no-boil) lasagna sheets

1 pound whole-milk low-moisture mozzarella cheese, freshly grated (about 3½ cups)

½ cup whole-milk ricotta cheese

¼ cup finely grated Parmigiano Reggiano cheese (preferably freshly grated)

¼ cup thinly sliced fresh basil leaves

---

1. Adjust an oven rack to the middle position and place a large sheet of aluminum foil on the rack below it to catch any drips from the pan above. Preheat the oven to 400°F.

2. Place the zucchini, onion, eggplant, olive oil, and salt in a large bowl and toss to combine. Turn the vegetables out onto a 10 x 16-inch rimmed sheet pan and roast until they begin to soften, about 15 minutes. Stir, then roast until the vegetables are tender and the zucchini begins to brown, about 15 minutes more. Transfer the vegetables to a heatproof bowl and set aside. (There's no need to wash the sheet pan.)

3. Reduce the oven temperature to 375°F. Place 1 cup tomato sauce in the bottom of the sheet pan you used to roast the vegetables and spread it out evenly with a spoon. Place enough sheets of pasta in the bottom of the sheet pan to form a single layer. (It's okay if they overlap slightly; for a 10 x 16-inch pan you'll use 6 sheets of pasta.) Spread another cup of tomato sauce over the pasta evenly. Sprinkle half the vegetables over the sauce followed by half the mozzarella cheese. Dollop heaping tablespoonfuls of ricotta cheese over the mozzarella. (It will spread during cooking.) Use all the ricotta in this layer.

4. Add another layer of pasta sheets, the remaining cup of tomato sauce, the remaining vegetables, and the remaining mozzarella cheese. Sprinkle the Parmigiano Reggiano cheese over the top. Bake until the cheese melts, about 25 minutes.

5. Preheat the broiler to high. Broil the lasagna until the cheese is browned, 3 to 5 minutes. Remove from the oven and cool for 5 to 10 minutes to firm up slightly before slicing. Sprinkle with the basil and serve.

# FRESH CORN CORNBREAD

*MAKES ABOUT 20 PIECES*

Due to the shallow depth of a sheet pan, this cornbread is not quite as cakelike as it might be if you baked it in a glass baking dish or cast-iron skillet. The benefits of using a sheet pan are that you get *more* cornbread, making this a great potluck recipe, plus, if you're a lover of crusts, this recipe has more browned surface and bottom and less spongy interior crumb than traditional cornbread. The coconut milk adds richness and a little sweetness. It's a slightly unexpected note that doesn't necessarily taste coconut-y, but adds to the overall depth of flavor—if you don't have any on hand, you can absolutely substitute whole milk. Fresh corn kernels are a nice and hearty addition, too—if corn isn't in season, skip it rather than using frozen corn.

---

1¼ cups all-purpose flour
1¼ cups fine cornmeal
2 teaspoons baking powder
½ teaspoon baking soda
1½ teaspoons kosher salt
½ cup (1 stick) unsalted butter, melted, plus 1 tablespoon at room temperature

2 large eggs
1 large egg yolk
½ cup granulated sugar
¾ cup coconut milk or whole milk
¾ cup sour cream
¼ cup honey
2 cups fresh corn kernels (cut from about 2 medium-size ears)

---

1. Adjust an oven rack to the middle position and preheat the oven to 350°F.

2. Whisk the flour, cornmeal, baking powder, baking soda, and salt in a medium-size bowl. Grease a 10 x 16-inch rimmed sheet pan with the room temperature butter and set aside.

3. Whisk the eggs, egg yolk, and sugar in a large bowl until creamy and frothy, about 1 minute. Add the coconut milk, sour cream, and honey and stir to combine, then whisk in the flour mixture. Add the melted butter and corn and stir until well combined. Pour this batter into the prepared sheet pan and even it out with an offset spatula.

4. Bake until a cake tester inserted in the center of the cornbread comes out clean and the cornbread resists light pressure, 20 to 22 minutes. Remove from the oven and cool slightly before slicing and serving.

# SMOKY EGGPLANT AND PROVOLONE PIZZA

SERVES 2 TO 4 (OR 1 IF YOU'RE REALLY HUNGRY!)

**I** really freaking love this pizza. It's just so, so, so good. The smoked paprika, ground fennel seed, and oregano make the eggplant take on a sausage-y taste without any of the heavy greasiness of actual sausage. The eggplant kind of melts into the cheese and other toppings, making the pizza more a sum of its parts than a vehicle for any single ingredient. With the onion, red bell pepper, and provolone, the flavor is even better than any sausage pizza. (And you know the deal about having to salt eggplant? You can skip it—it's not necessary; see page 50.) If you're not into eggplant, you can do the same thing with zucchini or quartered mushrooms for an equally great result.

8 ounces pizza dough
(homemade or store-bought)
¼ cup extra-virgin olive oil, plus extra
for rolling and drizzling
1¼ pounds eggplant (preferably
smaller eggplants like Italian or
Japanese), chopped into ½-inch
pieces
1 teaspoon smoked paprika
1 teaspoon ground fennel seed
1 teaspoon dried oregano
1½ teaspoons kosher salt
¼ teaspoon freshly ground black
pepper
½ small red onion, thinly sliced
into rings
1 cup freshly shredded provolone
cheese
¼ teaspoon crushed red pepper
flakes
2 tablespoons finely grated
Parmigiano Reggiano cheese
(preferably freshly grated)
8 fresh basil leaves

## Why Hand-Grating Cheese Matters

We've all done it—bought the pre-grated cheese at the store. It's such a time-saver and really, does it make *that* much of a difference? Well . . . yes it does! Pre-grated cheese rarely melts as well as freshly grated (unless you are buying cheese that was grated and packaged at a market and not by a big-brand company), especially if it includes these ingredients: starch to keep it from clumping, cellulose (which comes from wood pulp!) to act as a thickener and also prevent caking, and oftentimes an anti-mold agent to keep the cheese fresh for as long as possible. Why not just buy a block of cheese and grate it yourself? Not only will your food taste better, but you will know exactly what's in it.

enough, you can also simply stretch it out in the pan.) Cover with a damp kitchen towel and let it rest for 10 minutes.

3. Spread the vodka sauce over the pizza. (If you like a saucy pizza, use more; for a crisper crust, use less; I like to spread sauce and toppings to the edge of the dough.) Scatter the broccoli over the sauce, then sprinkle with a few pinches of salt. Sprinkle the mozzarella cheese over the broccoli and drizzle the remaining tablespoon olive oil over the top.

4. Bake until the cheese melts and just starts to brown, 12 to 15 minutes.

5. Sprinkle the Parmigiano Reggiano cheese over the pizza and return it to the oven. Turn the broiler to high and broil until the top of the pizza bubbles and begins to blister in spots, 2 to 3 minutes (watch the pizza closely as broiler intensities vary).

6. Remove the pizza from the oven and let it cool in the pan for 1 minute. With a spatula to help, pop the pizza out of the pan and slide it onto a cutting board. Slice into pieces and serve.

## Some Favorite Pizza Combos

Along with the sauce and your favorite cheese as a topper, try:

• Chopped mushrooms + rosemary + sweet onions (like Vidalia or Maui)

• Sliced red peppers + capers + sliced red onions

• Cauliflower florets + Gouda cheese (I like using half mozzarella and half Gouda) + chopped fresh thyme leaves

• Spinach + goat cheese + halved cherry tomatoes

• Chopped sweet potatoes + ricotta cheese + blue cheese

• Ribboned Swiss chard + sliced garlic + large egg cracked into the middle (It cooks while the pizza cooks!)

• Sliced white onions + sliced pickled jalapeño chiles + salsa

# SHAVED ZUCCHINI AND MINTY PESTO PIZZA

(V) *SERVES 2 TO 4 (OR 1 IF YOU'RE REALLY HUNGRY!)*

A traditional pesto contains cheese—either Parmigiano Reggiano or Pecorino Romano—but, here, for a lighter vegan-friendly take, I leave the cheese out with great results. Topped with seasoned raw zucchini ribbons, this pizza offers a nice combo of fresh vegetables and a baked pesto topping. If you'd like to make a cheesy pesto, add ¼ cup finely grated Pecorino Romano or Parmigiano Reggiano cheese to the food processor after adding the olive oil. I use all kinds of nuts to make pesto, from the traditional pine nuts to pistachios, walnuts, and even sunflower seeds. Feel free to experiment!

---

½ cup plus 3 tablespoons extra-virgin olive oil
8 ounces pizza dough (homemade or store-bought)
3 garlic cloves, roughly chopped
½ cup pine nuts
1 lemon, zested and halved
1¼ teaspoons kosher salt

2 cups (about 2 ounces) loosely packed fresh mint leaves plus 1 tablespoon finely chopped fresh mint leaves
1 medium-size zucchini, shaved into ribbons with a vegetable peeler
Flaky salt

---

1. Adjust an oven rack to the middle position and preheat the oven to 475°F. Lightly grease a half sheet pan with 1 tablespoon olive oil and set aside. Put the pizza dough on a lightly oiled cutting board and cover with a damp kitchen towel.

2. Combine the garlic, pine nuts, lemon zest, and 1 teaspoon salt in the bowl of a food processor and pulse 2 or 3 times to roughly chop and incorporate. Add 2 cups mint leaves and ½ cup olive oil and process until the mixture forms a paste. Scrape the pesto into a medium-size bowl.

3. Coat the pizza dough with 1 tablespoon olive oil and place it on your work surface. Roll the dough into a rustic oval shape, about ⅛ to ¼ inch thick, then place it in the sheet pan. (If your dough is soft enough, you can also simply stretch it out in the pan.) Cover with a damp kitchen towel and let it rest for 10 minutes.

4. Spread ⅓ cup pesto over the pizza (I like to let my toppings run all the way to the edge of the crust, but you can leave a border of ¾ inch bare if you like). Bake the pizza until the dough is golden brown, 12 to 15 minutes.

5. Meanwhile, place the zucchini in a medium-size bowl and toss with the remaining tablespoon mint, the remaining tablespoon olive oil, and the remaining ¼ teaspoon salt. With a spatula to help, pop the pizza out of the pan and slide it onto a cutting board. Top with the zucchini, squeeze a lemon half over the top, slice into pieces, and serve.

# BEAN, CHEESE, AND PICKLED JALAPEÑO BURRITZA

*SERVES 2 TO 4*

What's a burritza? It's essentially a burrito that uses pizza dough as the wrapper, instead of a tortilla, and eliminates the rice—because do you really need pizza dough *and* rice? (Maybe you think yes, but I think it's kind of crazy.) The bean and vegetable filling is sprinkled over the dough, then it's rolled up in a spiral and baked. You can serve it calzone style, in large pieces, or slice it crosswise into thin sections and serve it on its side, topped with a spoonful of guacamole (or more grated cheese and run it under the broiler for an extra-cheesy snack). However you choose, be sure to serve with plenty of spicy salsa!

1½ tablespoons extra-virgin olive oil, plus extra for the work surface
8 ounces pizza dough (homemade or store-bought)
1 cup cooked black beans or pinto beans, drained and rinsed
3 scallions, trimmed and finely chopped
½ cup finely chopped pickled jalapeño chiles
¼ cup finely chopped fresh cilantro leaves
3 tablespoons salsa (homemade, page 16 or 89, or store-bought), plus extra for serving
Kosher or other flaky salt, for sprinkling
1 cup freshly grated whole-milk low-moisture mozzarella cheese
½ teaspoon dried oregano

1. Adjust an oven rack to the middle position and preheat the oven to 400°F.

2. Coat the pizza dough with 1 tablespoon olive oil and place it on an oiled work surface. Roll and stretch the dough into a rectangle that is about ⅛ to ¼ inch thick. Cover with a damp kitchen towel and let it rest for 10 minutes.

3. Stir together the black beans, scallions, jalapeños, cilantro, and salsa in a medium-size bowl to combine.

**4.** Lightly roll the relaxed dough again so it is about ⅛ inch thick. Spread the bean mixture over the dough, leaving a 1-inch border at the top edge. Sprinkle with a few pinches of salt, then sprinkle the mozzarella cheese over the filling. Roll the pizza from the bottom edge up toward the top border to form a long cylinder. Pinch the seams shut along the bottom and sides.

**5.** Place the burritza on the sheet pan, seam-side down. (Bend it into a horseshoe shape or an *S* shape if it doesn't fit.) Brush the top with the remaining ½ tablespoon olive oil, then sprinkle with the oregano. Bake the burritza until the crust turns golden brown, 15 to 20 minutes.

**6.** Let the burritza cool on the pan for 1 minute. With a spatula to help, pop it out of the pan and slide it onto a cutting board. Let it rest for 5 minutes, then slice crosswise into 4 pieces and serve with extra salsa.

# CHEESY PIZZA TWISTS WITH ROASTED PEPPER MARINARA

*MAKES 8 TWISTS AND 2¼ CUPS MARINARA*

**A**s a mom, I like to inject as many vegetables as I can into sauces, especially when the sauces are destined for carb-heavy dishes like pasta or pizza. My boys go crazy for pizza parlor garlic knots—those fantastic little nubs of pizza dough slicked with garlic butter and flecked with a little parsley and grated Parmesan cheese. (Is it just a NYC thing?) I tap into that craving by making long, cheesy, buttery, ultra-garlicky twists that are super fun to dunk into a roasted pepper marinara on the side. I got the idea for combining mozzarella with Gouda cheese for bready twists from the brilliant baker Uri Scheft (of Breads Bakery in New York City and Lehamim in Tel Aviv). Coincidentally, this marinara is also awesome on pasta, and the twists are great alongside pasta, too, instead of garlic bread.

## FOR THE ROASTED PEPPER MARINARA

6 ripe plum tomatoes or small vine-ripened tomatoes, halved

2 red bell peppers, halved, stemmed, and seeded

4 garlic cloves, peeled

2 tablespoons extra-virgin olive oil

1 teaspoon kosher salt, plus extra as needed

1 tablespoon tomato paste

1½ teaspoons balsamic vinegar, plus extra as needed

Pinch of crushed red pepper flakes (optional)

## FOR THE PIZZA TWISTS

6 tablespoons unsalted butter

3 garlic cloves, minced

¼ teaspoon plus a pinch of kosher salt

1 large egg, lightly beaten

½ cup freshly grated whole-milk low-moisture mozzarella cheese

½ cup freshly grated Gouda cheese

1 pound pizza dough (homemade or store-bought)

All-purpose flour, for rolling

½ cup grated Parmigiano Reggiano cheese (preferably freshly grated)

1 tablespoon finely chopped fresh flat-leaf parsley leaves

1. Adjust an oven rack to the middle position and preheat the oven to 375°F. Line a rimmed sheet pan with parchment paper.

2. To make the roasted pepper marinara: Combine the tomato halves, red bell pepper halves, garlic, olive oil, and salt in a medium-size bowl and toss to combine. Transfer the tomatoes, cut side up, to the prepared pan. Add the bell peppers and garlic and scrape out every last drip of oil, drizzling it on top. Roast the vegetables until they are very juicy, 40 to 45 minutes (if they brown too much, tent them loosely with aluminum foil). Increase the oven temperature to 425°F.

3. Transfer the roasted vegetables to a blender or food processor, being sure to scrape all the juices in, too. (Discard the parchment and set the pan aside for later.) Add the tomato paste, balsamic vinegar, and crushed red pepper flakes (if using) and pulse until smooth. Taste and adjust the seasoning with a pinch of salt or more balsamic vinegar if needed. Set aside or refrigerate until serving (warm before serving).

4. To make the pizza twists: Place the butter and garlic in a microwave-safe bowl. Microwave until the butter is completely melted, about 1 minute, stopping the microwave every 20 seconds to stir the butter. Stir in ¼ teaspoon salt and set aside.

5. With a fork, beat the egg with 1 tablespoon water and a pinch of salt in a medium-size bowl and set aside. With your fingers, toss the mozzarella and Gouda cheeses together in a separate medium-size bowl.

6. Place a fresh sheet of parchment on the sheet pan you used for the vegetables. On a lightly floured work surface, roll the dough into a rectangle, 10 inches long and 8 inches wide (with the short side facing you). Brush the dough with the egg wash, sprinkle the cheese mixture on top, and press it down firmly. Slice the dough vertically into eight (1-inch-wide) strips. Twist each strip twice (so it has at least 3 turns) and place it on the prepared sheet pan. Repeat with the remaining dough pieces, placing them about 1 inch apart. Dip a clean pastry brush into the garlic butter and dab it over the length of each twist, using half the garlic butter. Sprinkle with half the Parmigiano Reggiano cheese.

7. Bake the twists until they are golden brown, 15 to 18 minutes. Remove from the oven, dab with the remaining garlic butter, and immediately sprinkle with the remaining Parmigiano Reggiano cheese and the parsley. Serve with the roasted pepper marinara on the side for dipping.

# POTATO, ROSEMARY, AND ROASTED GARLIC FOCACCIA

Ⓥ *SERVES 6 TO 8*

There's something about crispy, garlicky potatoes on bread that just tastes so indulgent and so good. In this recipe garlic cloves are slow-poached in olive oil with rosemary, and that oil is then used to season the potatoes before they are layered over pizza dough. Focaccia dough is usually made a little differently than pizza dough but, for this version, I just use a doubled quantity of pizza dough so it creates a thicker layer of focaccia in the bottom of the pan.

---

1 pound pizza dough (homemade or store-bought)
4 large garlic cloves, peeled and roughly chopped
2 teaspoons fresh rosemary leaves, roughly chopped
5 tablespoons extra-virgin olive oil, plus extra for drizzling

1½ teaspoons kosher salt
1 large Yukon Gold potato, unpeeled, very thinly sliced into $\frac{1}{16}$- to $\frac{1}{8}$-inch-thick rounds (use a mandoline if you have one)
¼ teaspoon freshly ground black pepper

---

1. Adjust one oven rack to the middle position and another to the upper-middle position and preheat the oven to 400°F. Put the pizza dough on a lightly oiled cutting board and cover with a damp kitchen towel.

2. Combine the garlic and rosemary in a ramekin and cover with ¼ cup olive oil. Cover the ramekin with aluminum foil and place it in the oven. Bake on the middle rack until the garlic is very soft and fragrant, about 20 minutes. Remove the ramekin from the oven and set aside.

3. Grease a 10 x 16-inch sheet pan with 1 tablespoon olive oil. Place the dough in the pan and press, push, and pull with your fingers so it fills the pan evenly. Cover with a damp kitchen towel and let it rest for 10 minutes.

4. Strain the garlic oil through a fine-mesh sieve and into a medium-size bowl, reserving the garlic and

rosemary. Dip your fingers into the garlic oil and press them into the dough to create deep dimples all over. With a fork, mash the garlic and rosemary together into a rough paste. With your fingers, dab the garlic-rosemary mixture evenly over the dough, then dip your fingers back into the garlic oil, and press them into the dough again to re-create the indentations. Sprinkle the surface with ½ teaspoon salt.

5. Add the potatoes to the bowl with the remaining garlic oil, ¾ teaspoon salt, and the pepper and toss to coat evenly. Lay the potato slices on top of the dough, overlapping them slightly like shingles on a roof. Drizzle with any garlic oil left in the bowl and sprinkle with the remaining ¼ teaspoon salt.

6. Bake on the middle rack until the potatoes are golden brown and the focaccia is browned around the edges, 22 to 26 minutes.

7. Turn the broiler to high and move the focaccia to the upper-middle rack. Broil until the potatoes are crisp, 3 to 5 minutes (watch the potatoes closely as broiler intensities vary).

8. Remove the focaccia from the oven. Cool for 15 minutes before sliding a metal spatula under the focaccia to lift it from the pan and slide it onto a cutting board. Slice the focaccia into squares and serve warm or at room temperature.

Chapter 7

# BREAKFASTS AND BRUNCHES

The art of breakfast can be as simple (almond butter and apples on bread) or as elaborate (Slab Quiche with Spinach, Goat Cheese, and Caramelized Onions, page 186, here's looking at you) as you make it. Here, I put together a wish-list roster of some of my favorite breakfast dishes, from A Perfect Avocado Toast (page 174), which I have at least four times a week, no joke) to a wonderfully rich Eggs in Guajillo Chile Sauce (page 183), and Granola Banana Bread (page 195) invigorated by the addition of granola to the batter. A sheet pan is so versatile it can handle all these recipes with ease. A standard half sheet will work nine times out of ten, but for the frittata, slab quiche, breakfast cake, and banana bread, it's best to find a pan that matches—as closely as possible—the dimensions called for in the recipe.

# A PERFECT AVOCADO TOAST

(V)  *MAKES 2 PIECES*

Listen: I wrote the book on toast (quite literally . . . I did!), so when I say this is a stellar toast, you'd better believe it is. It's like salad for breakfast, but even better because there's none of that pesky lettuce to get in the way of the goodies—avocado; flaky salt; and ripe, luscious tomatoes. (I think my stomach just growled.) The tahini sauce adds a little extra bit of decadence (and fiber and potassium and and and . . . see page 26), but you can leave it off if you don't have the eight seconds it takes to make it. (Note the sarcasm?)

2 slices (each ½ to ¾ inch thick)
    best-quality bread
2 tablespoons extra-virgin olive oil
Flaky sea salt, for sprinkling and
    seasoning
2 tablespoons tahini (sesame paste)
Squeeze of fresh lemon juice

1 small cucumber, chopped into bite-
    size pieces
1 medium-size ripe tomato, chopped
    into bite-size pieces
1 perfectly ripe avocado, halved and
    pitted
Freshly ground black pepper,
    for seasoning

1. Adjust an oven rack to the top position and preheat the broiler to high.

2. Place the bread on a rimmed sheet pan and drizzle 1 tablespoon olive oil over the 2 slices. Sprinkle with salt and toast until golden brown (watch the bread closely as broiler intensities vary), 2 to 3 minutes. Turn the bread and toast the other side, about 1 minute. (I like to keep the second side less toasted so the toast isn't brittle and too crunchy.) Transfer both pieces of toast to a plate.

3. Whisk the tahini paste with 1 tablespoon cold water and the lemon juice in a small bowl. Add a generous pinch of salt, taste, and add more water or salt if needed. Add the cucumber and tomato and toss to combine.

4. Scoop an avocado half onto each bread slice and smash it down with a fork. Sprinkle with salt. Divide the salad over the top of each piece of toast. Drizzle the remaining tablespoon of olive oil over both slices, sprinkle with salt, and add a grind of pepper. Serve immediately.

# GINGERED APPLE AND ALMOND BUTTER TOAST

**VO** *MAKES 4 PIECES*

A pples tossed in honey and spices and roasted under the broiler make a wonderfully warm and sweet apple pie–like topping for a protein-rich almond butter–swiped piece of toast. I like making toast under the broiler because spreading butter on bread before toasting allows the fat to seep into the nooks of the bread, creating little flavor pockets of goodness, while the natural sugars in the butter caramelize a bit thanks to the sear of the broiler.

---

2 crisp, sweet apples, peeled, cored, and cut into ¼-inch slices
2 tablespoons honey
½ teaspoon ground cinnamon
½ teaspoon ground ginger
⅛ teaspoon ground allspice or ground cloves

⅛ teaspoon kosher salt
4 slices good-quality bread (each about ¾ inch thick)
2 tablespoons unsalted butter, at room temperature
½ cup almond butter
Flaky salt, for sprinkling (optional)

---

1. Adjust an oven rack to the upper-middle position and preheat the broiler to high. Line a rimmed sheet pan with parchment paper or a silicone baking mat.

2. Place the apples in a large bowl and toss with the honey, cinnamon, ginger, allspice, and kosher salt. Arrange the apples on the prepared sheet pan and roast until tender and the honey begins to caramelize around the edges of the apples, 5 to 7 minutes (watch the apples closely as broiler intensities vary). Transfer the apples to a bowl and set aside.

3. Spread one side of each piece of bread with the butter. Place the slices on a rimmed sheet pan, buttered-side up, and broil until toasted, 2 to 3 minutes (watch it closely—few things are worse than burnt toast!). Flip the bread and lightly toast the other side, 1 to 2 minutes longer. Transfer the toast to 4 plates.

4. Spread the buttered side of each piece of toast with 2 tablespoons almond butter. Sprinkle with a pinch of flaky salt (if using) and arrange the apples over the top. Serve warm or at room temperature.

# ROASTED STRAWBERRY DANISH

*MAKES 4 DANISHES*

I love making these on weekends for my two sons when they're craving a fresh-baked croissant but I'm craving a morning of laziness in bed and not an early run to the corner bakery. If you have English muffins, cream cheese, and strawberries, you can make these in a snap! You can skip roasting the strawberries if you like and just use jam in the center instead, but I beg you not to because roasted strawberries have the ability to, oh, you know, change your life and all—ladled over ice cream, swirled into muffin batter, layered with yogurt and granola, blended into smoothies, spooned over pancakes. . . . The Danish is the dish but the strawberries are the *dish* if you catch my drift.

---

2 cups (1 pint) fresh strawberries, hulled and halved
6 tablespoons sugar
¾ cup all-purpose flour
¼ teaspoon kosher salt
4 tablespoons (½ stick) cold unsalted butter, cut into very small pieces

⅔ cup cream cheese, softened slightly
1 teaspoon fresh lemon juice
¼ cup confectioners' sugar, plus extra for dusting (optional)
2 English muffins, halved and toasted

---

1. Adjust an oven rack to the middle position and preheat the oven to 350°F. Line a rimmed sheet pan with parchment paper and set it aside.

2. Toss the strawberries and 2 tablespoons sugar in a medium-size bowl. Turn the strawberries out onto the prepared sheet pan and turn them all cut side up. Roast until they are soft and juicy, about 20 minutes. Remove from the oven and return the strawberries to the bowl. Discard the parchment paper and set the sheet pan aside.

3. Meanwhile, whisk the flour, remaining 3 tablespoons sugar, and the salt in a medium-size bowl. Add the butter pieces and, with your fingers, work the butter into the dry ingredients until the mixture forms a sandy streusel with some chunky pea-size pieces.

4. In a separate medium-size bowl, stir together the cream cheese and lemon juice. Place the confectioners' sugar in a sieve and sift it into the cream cheese; stir until smooth. Reduce the oven temperature to 325°F.

5. Divide the cream cheese mixture among the toasted English muffin halves, spreading it evenly. Make a well in the center of the cream cheese mixture and add some strawberries to it, then sprinkle the streusel around the edges of the cream cheese–topped muffin halves.

6. Return the sheet pan to the oven and bake until the streusel becomes golden, 12 to 15 minutes. Remove from the oven and cool slightly before serving. Dust with more confectioners' sugar, if you like.

# ROASTED FRUIT, PUMPKIN SEED, AND YOGURT BOWLS

VO GF  *SERVES 4*

O h, hi, roasted fruit. Wait, you've never roasted fruit? Not even for a Danish (page 176) or as a topping for luscious mascarpone cheese (page 233)? It's the best way to turn ho-hum, less-than-perfectly-ripe produce into a "Yowza, that's good!" experience. You can roast just about any kind of fruit to make these fruit bowls (see the Variations), and if you're not down with caramelized pumpkin seeds, try toasted almonds or pistachios instead.

If you are using blueberries in combination with another fruit, add them during the last 10 minutes of roasting, or, if using blueberries only, roast them for just 10 minutes. If you're using apples and pears, they may need a few extra minutes to roast and become tender.

---

6 tablespoons pumpkin seeds
½ tablespoon unsalted butter, melted
2½ tablespoons sugar
Pinch of flaky salt
4 cups fresh fruit, such as apples, bananas, blueberries, halved and pitted cherries, mangos, nectarines, peaches, pears, pineapples, plums, rhubarb, or strawberries; larger fruits cut into attractive 1- to 2-bite pieces (see Variations, next page)
3 tablespoons honey
3 cups plain Greek yogurt (full fat, reduced fat, or 0%)

---

1. Adjust an oven rack to the middle position and preheat the oven to 400°F. Line a rimmed sheet pan with parchment paper.

2. Place the pumpkin seeds on the prepared sheet pan, drizzle them with the melted butter, sprinkle with ½ tablespoon sugar, and toss to coat. Add a pinch of salt and stir to combine. Roast the pumpkin seeds until toasted, 7 to 9 minutes. Remove from the oven, lift off the parchment (and seeds), and place on a plate to cool.

3. Place a fresh piece of parchment on the sheet pan. Add the fruit to the pan and drizzle with the honey and remaining 2 tablespoons sugar. Roast the fruit until it's juicy (some types of fruit will caramelize and

some may not—big flavor bonus if it does!), 15 to 20 minutes. Remove from the oven and transfer the fruit and any juices from the pan to a bowl.

4. Dollop a large spoonful of the yogurt into each of 4 bowls (stemless wine glasses work well, too). Top with the fruit and some of their juices. Serve sprinkled with pumpkin seeds.

## VARIATIONS

Some of my favorite roasted fruit combinations are:

**Strawberries + Rhubarb**
**Bananas + Mangos**
**Pineapple + Raspberries**
**Cherries + Plums**

# LOADED CHILAQUILES WITH BAKED EGGS

*SERVES 2*

I'm going to try to pretend that chilaquiles are *not* nachos disguised as breakfast. I mean, they're not covered with cheese—just a spare sprinkle of crumbly, salty Mexican Cotija (ricotta salata or even feta works in a pinch). Traditionally the chips are bathed in either a green or red sauce (like the Guajillo Chile Sauce on page 183—which you can use if you like). Here, I use the bright and punchy Charred Tomatillo Salsa (page 16) to soften the chips. I also add some vegetable goodness—and amazing flavor—by roasting poblanos, onion, and jalapeño. Usually the egg that accompanies chilaquiles is fried on the side, which you can totally do if you don't have a ramekin but, as your oven is on anyway, why not kill two birds with one sheet pan?

---

2 poblano chiles, stemmed, halved, seeded, and sliced lengthwise into thin strips

1 medium-size red onion, halved and thinly sliced

1 medium-size jalapeño chile, thinly sliced into rounds (see Note)

2 tablespoons extra-virgin olive oil, plus extra for the ramekins

¾ teaspoon kosher salt, plus extra for sprinkling

½ teaspoon ground cumin

½ teaspoon freshly ground black pepper

7 cups tortilla chips

2½ cups Charred Tomatillo Salsa (page 16) or store-bought tomatillo salsa

2 large eggs

½ cup crumbled Cotija cheese

½ cup roughly chopped fresh cilantro leaves

---

1. Adjust an oven rack to the middle position and preheat the oven to 400°F.

2. Toss the poblanos, red onion, jalapeño, olive oil, salt, cumin, and pepper together in a large bowl. Transfer to a rimmed sheet pan and roast, stirring midway through cooking, until the onion starts to brown, about 25 minutes. Transfer the vegetables back to the bowl.

3. Add the tortilla chips and tomatillo sauce to the vegetables and toss to combine. Transfer the tortilla chips

to the sheet pan and spread them into a somewhat even and not too tall layer that covers about three-fourths of the pan. Lightly grease 2 ramekins with olive oil and crack an egg into each. Sprinkle a little salt over the top. Put the pan in the oven and place the ramekins on the side without chips. Bake until the eggs are cooked through and the chips are warmed, 10 to 12 minutes.

4. Remove the sheet pan from the oven. Divide the chips between 2 plates. Make a well in the center of each mound and carefully slide an egg into it. Sprinkle the eggs with salt, then sprinkle everything with the Cotija cheese and cilantro, and serve hot.

NOTE: If you prefer things on the milder side, halve, seed, and finely chop the jalapeño chile for less heat.

# EGGS IN GUAJILLO CHILE SAUCE

**GF** *SERVES 4*

Okay, disclaimer: This is not a Wednesday morning slap-and-dash breakfast-before-work kind of situation. Not to say it's complicated—it just takes a moment of time and a nod of effort. You have to roast the dried chiles, encouraging their smoky flavor to develop and heighten, and then soak them and coax them into a soft state so they can be blended with roasted tomatoes and garlic and herbs. The sauce is reduced a little in the oven before the eggs are poached in there, too. The result is kind of like eggs in purgatory with a Latin shimmy. (See page 79 for another tasty use of the Guajillo Chile Sauce—a Tortilla Rojo Bake!)

---

8 dried guajillo chiles
   (about 2 ounces; see Note)
1 dried ancho chile
1½ cups boiling water
1 pound plum tomatoes,
   halved lengthwise
¼ cup extra-virgin olive oil
3½ teaspoons kosher salt,
   plus extra for sprinkling
1 can (14 ounces) chopped tomatoes
   (preferably fire roasted)
4 garlic cloves, roughly chopped

1 tablespoon dark brown sugar
1 teaspoon dried oregano
1 teaspoon ground cumin
½ teaspoon ground coriander
2 cups vegetable broth or water
8 large eggs
Crumbled Cotija cheese (optional)
½ cup finely chopped fresh cilantro
   leaves
Warmed corn tortillas or toast,
   for serving (see box, page 184)
Lime wedges, for serving

---

1. Adjust an oven rack to the middle position and preheat the oven to 375°F.

2. Place a wire cooling rack inside a rimmed sheet pan and place the guajillo and ancho chiles on the rack. Roast the chiles until they are fragrant and begin to darken, 4 to 5 minutes. Transfer the chiles to a medium-size bowl and cover with the boiling water. Put a plate on the chiles to submerge them and set the bowl aside for 20 minutes.

3. Increase the oven temperature to 400°F. Remove the wire rack from the sheet pan and line the pan with a piece of parchment paper. Toss the tomatoes with 2 tablespoons olive oil

and 1½ teaspoons salt in a medium-size bowl, then place them on the sheet pan, cut side up. Roast until they are juicy, about 30 minutes. Remove the pan from the oven and transfer the tomatoes to a blender.

4. Remove the chiles from the water (save the water in the bowl). Discard the stems and slice the chiles open lengthwise. Scrape away the seeds and add the chiles to the blender, along with 1 cup of the reserved soaking water, the canned tomatoes, the garlic, sugar, oregano, cumin, coriander, and remaining 2 teaspoons salt. Blend at medium speed until very smooth. Return the sheet pan to the oven to heat it.

5. Add the remaining 2 tablespoons olive oil to the heated pan and pour in the guajillo sauce. (It should sizzle.) Return the pan to the oven, stirring every 5 minutes, until the mixture becomes very thick and pasty, about 10 minutes. Stir in the vegetable broth and continue to bake until the sauce is thick and lush, about 15 minutes.

6. Crack the eggs into the sauce and return the pan to the oven. Bake until the whites are set and the yolks are still soft, about 7 minutes for a soft yolk and 9 minutes for a medium-cooked yolk. Remove from the oven, sprinkle with salt, and divide among 4 plates. Sprinkle with Cotija cheese (if using), and cilantro, and serve with tortillas and lime wedges on the side.

**NOTE:** Guajillo chiles are the dried version of the mirasol chile pepper. They are a deep scarlet color and, generally, 1½ to 2 inches wide and 2½ to 4 inches long. They have a mild, sweet, fruity flavor. A pasilla chile or ancho chile can be used as a substitute.

## No Excuse Not to Warm Them Up!

When it comes to tortillas, warmth makes all the difference—heating tortillas makes them more pliable and brings out their otherwise subtle flavor. Plus, it's easy to do:

**ON THE STOVETOP (USING A GAS BURNER):** Set your gas burner to medium heat. Place the tortilla directly on the burner and, with tongs, flip the tortilla every 15 to 20 seconds until warm, pliable, and a little singed around the edges.

**IN A SKILLET:** Heat a dry cast-iron skillet over medium-high heat. Warm the tortillas, one at a time, until each side is warmed and the tortilla is pliable, 1½ to 2 minutes per tortilla. Wrap loosely in a clean kitchen towel while warming the remaining tortillas.

**IN THE MICROWAVE:** Wrap a stack of tortillas in a double layer of damp paper towels and microwave at high power in 30-second bursts until the tortillas are warmed through.

# SLAB FRITTATA WITH LEEKS, MUSHROOMS, AND RICOTTA CHEESE

GF *SERVES 6 TO 8*

I first had a frittata baked in a sheet pan in Parma, Italy. It was baked by a very well-lived, wise woman who, no doubt, had cooked this at least a thousand times over her life. It was deliciously brilliant—a great brunchy dish for a crowd. She sliced it into small squares and served it with a generous smile.

---

- 2 medium-size leeks, white and light green parts only, halved, rinsed well to remove any grit, and thinly sliced
- ½ pound shiitake mushrooms, stemmed and thinly sliced
- 1 tablespoon finely chopped fresh rosemary leaves
- 2 garlic cloves, minced
- 3 tablespoons extra-virgin olive oil
- 1¼ teaspoons kosher salt
- 12 large eggs, lightly beaten
- 3 tablespoons unsalted butter, melted
- ¾ cup heavy (whipping) cream
- ½ cup finely grated Parmigiano Reggiano cheese
- ½ teaspoon freshly ground black pepper
- ½ cup ricotta cheese

---

1. Adjust an oven rack to the middle position and preheat the oven to 350°F.

2. Toss together the leeks, mushrooms, rosemary, garlic, olive oil, and ½ teaspoon salt in a medium-size bowl. Turn the vegetables out onto a rimmed sheet pan and roast, stirring midway through cooking, until the mushrooms are tender and the leeks are caramelized, about 20 to 25 minutes. Remove the sheet pan from the oven and set it aside.

3. Whisk the eggs with the butter, cream, and remaining ¾ teaspoon salt in a small bowl until the eggs are frothy. Whisk in the Parmigiano Reggiano cheese and pepper to combine.

4. Ladle the egg mixture over the vegetables. Dollop the ricotta cheese over the top. Place the sheet pan in the oven and bake until the eggs are set and don't jiggle in the middle when the pan is tapped, 15 to 18 minutes. Remove from the oven, slice into pieces, and serve warm or at room temperature.

# SLAB QUICHE WITH SPINACH, GOAT CHEESE, AND CARAMELIZED ONIONS

*SERVES 4 TO 6*

**M**y favorite way to entertain is to invite a bunch of friends over and lay everything out on the dining table: vegetables, pasta, quiche, breads, grains—you name it. I put out plates and forks and decorate the table with candles and cute seasonal vegetables—baby pumpkins and bouquets of sage in the fall, bunches of mint and carrots in the spring, bowlfuls of citrus fruit in the winter, and little fairytale eggplant or bright red cherry tomatoes in the summer. It's casual and fun, and encourages everyone to eat, drink, and socialize at will. Quiche is an ideal player for this kind of setup—it can be served warm or at room temperature and is just as happy on a brunch spread as it is at dinner or in the afternoon with tea.

---

1 medium-size red onion, halved and thinly sliced
3 tablespoons extra-virgin olive oil
1 teaspoon finely chopped fresh thyme leaves
1 teaspoon kosher salt
All-purpose flour, for rolling
1 sheet thawed frozen puff pastry
2 large eggs plus 2 large egg yolks
1 cup whole milk

½ cup heavy (whipping) cream
½ teaspoon freshly ground black pepper
1½ cups freshly grated Gruyère cheese
2 cups roughly chopped fresh spinach
4 ounces fresh goat cheese, crumbled (about ½ cup)

---

**1.** Adjust an oven rack to the lower-middle position and preheat the oven to 300°F.

**2.** Place the red onion on a rimmed 10 x 16-inch pan and drizzle with olive oil. Toss with the thyme and spread into an even layer. Cover the sheet pan with aluminum foil

(you may need 2 sheets), crimping it tightly around the edges to seal, and roast the onions until they are soft, about 20 minutes. Uncover the pan, stir, and continue to cook until the onions are very soft, sticky, and golden brown, 15 to 20 minutes more. Remove the sheet pan from the oven, sprinkle the onions with ½ teaspoon salt, and transfer them to a plate to cool completely (reserve the sheet pan and any grease or seasonings left in it for Step 4).

3. Increase the oven temperature to 400°F.

4. Lightly flour your work surface and put the puff pastry on top. Lightly roll out the pastry to between ⅛ and ¼ inch thick. Transfer the pastry to the reserved sheet pan—it should just cover the bottom. With a fork, prick the dough all over, then place the sheet pan in the refrigerator while you make the filling.

5. Whisk the whole eggs and egg yolks to combine in a large bowl. Whisk in the milk and cream, and add the remaining ½ teaspoon salt, and the pepper. Remove the crust from the refrigerator and sprinkle half the Gruyère over it. Add the onions in an even layer and then the spinach followed by the remaining Gruyère. Pour the egg filling over and crumble the goat cheese over the top.

6. Bake the quiche for 10 minutes. Reduce the oven temperature to 375°F and continue to bake until the filling is set around the edges and bounces back to light pressure in the center, 20 to 25 minutes.

7. Turn the broiler on to high and adjust an oven rack to the top position. Move the quiche to the top rack and broil until browned, about 1 minute (watch the quiche closely as broiler intensities vary). Remove from the oven, slice, and serve warm or at room temperature.

# BREAKFAST RICE BOWL WITH RAISINS AND ALMONDS

(V) (GF)  SERVES 4 TO 6

This is like rice pudding meets morning hot porridge. It's warm and homey and comforting and a nice switch from oatmeal (page 191) if you're a warm cereal lover. For a sweeter vibe that could even stand in for dessert, finish the rice bowl with a drizzle of condensed milk (or even condensed coconut milk!).

---

2 cups short-grain white rice, such as sushi rice or arborio rice

3 cups boiling almond, coconut, or rice milk, plus extra warm milk for serving

½ cup raisins

½ cup slivered almonds

2½ teaspoons sugar

½ teaspoon ground cinnamon

Maple syrup, for serving

---

1. Adjust an oven rack to the middle position and preheat the oven to 400°F.

2. Put the rice on a rimmed sheet pan and place the pan on the oven rack. Add the boiling almond milk, followed by the raisins, almonds, sugar, and cinnamon, and, with a fork, stir to combine, spreading the rice as evenly as possible. Cover the sheet pan with aluminum foil (you may need 2 sheets), crimping it tightly around the edges to seal.

3. Reduce the oven temperature to 350°F and bake until the rice is tender and most (or all) of the milk is absorbed, 20 to 22 minutes.

4. Remove the sheet pan from the oven and divide the rice among bowls. Finish each with a splash of warm almond milk and a drizzle of maple syrup.

## Homespun Syrups

There's a saying I like to dish out when someone asks me if I want sugar in my coffee, honey in my tea, maple in my oatmeal: "Life is bitter enough—I'll take the sweetness, thanks!" Here are some simple and fun ways to create homemade syrups and sugars to add a bit of joy to oatmeal, rice porridge, pancakes, morning yogurt—you name it. Plus, packaged in a Mason jar with a bit of twine and a cute tag, they make a great hostess/host/housewarming/just-because gift.

**BLUEBERRY MAPLE:** Heat fresh or frozen blueberries with maple syrup in a small saucepan for a few minutes until the blueberries soften and leach their color.

**GINGER HONEY:** Heat the honey with a few slices of fresh ginger until the mixture becomes fragrant. Remove the ginger before serving (add a few fresh sage leaves or a sprig of fresh rosemary, if you like).

**STRAWBERRY SYRUP:** Bring ½ cup sugar and ½ cup water to a boil in a small saucepan. Add some chopped strawberries and a spoonful or two of strawberry jam and simmer until the strawberries soften.

# BAKED OATMEAL WITH DATES, BANANAS, AND TAHINI SYRUP

V GF *SERVES 4*

Baking oats makes sense because you don't have to worry about scorching them—the oven provides beautifully even heat and makes your morning oatmeal relatively hands-off easy. The steel-cut oats need to be soaked the night before you want to eat them so, in the morning, all you need to do is stir in the tasty extras before popping them in the oven to bake.

## FOR THE OATMEAL

1 cup steel-cut oats
4 cups boiling water
¼ teaspoon kosher salt
1 cup full-fat or lite coconut milk
2 bananas, cut into bite-size pieces
1 cup pitted dates, roughly chopped
½ cup granola, homemade or store-
  bought (optional)

## FOR THE TAHINI SYRUP

¼ cup tahini (sesame paste), plus
  extra as needed
2 tablespoons maple syrup or honey,
  plus extra as needed
Pinch of flaky salt

1. To make the oatmeal: Spread the oats on a rimmed sheet pan and add the boiling water and salt. Cover the pan with aluminum foil and set aside overnight.

2. Adjust an oven rack to the middle position and preheat the oven to 350°F.

3. Add the coconut milk, bananas, and dates to the oatmeal and stir to combine. Cover the pan with aluminum foil (you may need 2 sheets), crimping it tightly around the edges to seal, and bake for 20 minutes. Uncover the pan and continue to bake until the oatmeal is thick, about 15 minutes longer. Turn off the oven (leave the oatmeal inside the oven so it thickens more).

4. To make the tahini syrup: Whisk the tahini with ¼ cup water, the maple syrup, and salt. Taste and add more sweetener or tahini (for a thicker syrup) if needed.

5. Divide the oatmeal among 4 bowls. Drizzle with tahini syrup. Sprinkle with granola (if using) and serve.

# ZUCCHINI BREAKFAST CAKE WITH PECAN-COCONUT STREUSEL

V · *MAKES ABOUT 12 PIECES*

This twist on zucchini bread gets a bit of heartiness from cornmeal and moisture from oats. To keep the zucchini from leaching too much liquid into the batter as the cake bakes, I like to toss it with sugar before adding it to the batter (it works the same as tossing vegetables with salt—the sugar helps to pull out moisture). The oats help to keep the cake nice and moist, making it a good one to bake on Sunday and snack on all week long.

---

1 medium-size (½ pound) zucchini, grated on the medium-size holes of a box grater (about 1½ cups)
½ cup plus 1 tablespoon sugar
⅓ cup coconut oil, melted, plus 1 tablespoon for coating the pan
1¼ cups all-purpose flour
¾ cup fine cornmeal
½ cup quick-cooking oats
1 cup pecan pieces, finely chopped

¾ cup confectioners' sugar
1½ teaspoons baking soda
½ teaspoon kosher salt
1½ cups lite coconut milk
¾ cup packed light brown sugar
¼ cup maple syrup
1 teaspoon distilled white vinegar
2 teaspoons pure vanilla extract
½ cup unsweetened coconut flakes

---

1. Toss the zucchini with 1 tablespoon sugar in a small bowl. Transfer to a fine-mesh sieve and place over the sink or a bowl so the zucchini can drain.

2. Adjust an oven rack to the middle position and preheat the oven to 350°F. Grease a 10 x 16-inch rimmed sheet pan with 1 tablespoon coconut oil. Line the pan with a large sheet of parchment paper, pressing it into place, then flip the paper, and press it into the pan so both sides are greased.

3. Whisk the flour, cornmeal, oats, ½ cup pecans, ¼ cup confectioners' sugar, the baking soda, and salt in a large bowl.

4. Whisk the coconut milk, brown sugar, remaining ½ cup sugar, remaining ⅓ cup coconut oil, maple syrup, vinegar, and vanilla in a medium-size bowl.

5. Stir together the remaining ½ cup pecans and the coconut flakes in a small bowl and set aside. Squeeze out as much liquid as possible from the zucchini.

6. Pour the coconut milk mixture over the flour mixture, add the zucchini, and stir to combine. Pour the batter into the prepared sheet pan, spreading it evenly. Sprinkle the pecan-coconut topping evenly over the batter.

7. Bake until a cake tester inserted into the center of the cake comes out clean, about 20 minutes. Remove the cake from the oven and set it aside to cool for at least 30 minutes before slicing into squares and serving. Store leftover cake in an airtight container for up to 5 days.

# GRANOLA BANANA BREAD

*MAKES ABOUT 12 PIECES*

S ometimes the best recipes happen by accident. I was at a friend's country house one summer morning and got the urge to bake. I decided to wing it and challenge myself by not opening a cookbook to reference a recipe. I spotted a Mason jar of yummy-looking granola and was curious what it would taste like baked into a quick bread. I got my answer when we couldn't stop snacking on the bread (even a little country mouse got into the action). Use any kind of granola you like—there are two recipes in this book (page 197 or page 199) or use your favorite store-bought brand.

---

1½ cups slivered almonds
  (or any nuts)
1 tablespoon unsalted butter,
  at room temperature
1½ cups whole-wheat flour
1½ cups all-purpose flour
1 cup granola
1 tablespoon ground cinnamon
2 teaspoons baking powder
1 teaspoon kosher salt

¾ teaspoon baking soda
4 large eggs
1 tablespoon pure vanilla extract
1½ cups packed light brown sugar
¾ cup sugar
¾ cup canola oil
¾ cup extra-virgin olive oil
4 medium-size ripe bananas,
  well smashed

---

1. Adjust an oven rack to the middle position and preheat the oven to 350°F.

2. Spread the almonds on a rimmed sheet pan and toast in the oven until golden, shaking the pan occasionally, 8 to 9 minutes. Set aside to cool.

3. Line a 10 x 16-inch rimmed sheet pan with parchment paper and coat with the butter.

4. Whisk the whole-wheat flour, all-purpose flour, granola, cinnamon, baking powder, salt, and baking soda in a large bowl. Set aside.

5. Crack 2 eggs into another large bowl. Separate the other 2 eggs, cracking the whites into a medium-size bowl and adding the yolks to the bowl with the whole eggs. Vigorously whisk the egg whites until they are stiff; set them aside. To the 2 whole eggs plus 2 egg yolks add the brown

## Freezing Fruit

When I have fruit that is extra ripe, and perhaps a little too ripe to eat out of hand, I freeze it to use in syrups, smoothies, jams, or quick breads. Here's a quick look at how:

**BANANAS:** Peel away and discard the skin. Store the bananas in a freezer-safe resealable bag.

**BERRIES:** Place them on a plate or sheet pan in the freezer for about 30 minutes (if using strawberries, hull and halve them first). Once semi-frozen, transfer the berries to a freezer-safe resealable bag.

**PINEAPPLE:** Cut into bite-size pieces and place them on a plate or sheet pan in the freezer for about 30 minutes. Once semi-frozen, transfer to a freezer-safe resealable bag.

**PEACHES AND NECTARINES:** Halve, pit, and cut into bite-size pieces. Place them on a plate or sheet pan in the freezer for about 30 minutes. Once semi-frozen, transfer to a freezer-safe resealable bag.

sugar and sugar and whisk until pale and creamy, about 1 minute. Add the canola and olive oils and whisk until combined, then whisk in the bananas. Add the flour mixture and the cooled almonds and whisk until hardly any dry streaks remain. Fold in the whipped egg whites.

6. Spread the batter evenly into the prepared sheet pan and bake until a cake tester inserted into the center of the cake comes out clean and the cake resists light pressure, 16 to 18 minutes. Cool completely before cutting and serving.

# PUMPKIN SEED–APPLE GRANOLA

(V) (GF) *MAKES 4 CUPS*

Good granola—made with quality ingredients and that doesn't taste like sugary cereal in disguise—can be super pricey. It's much more satisfying to make your own. Plus it's EASY. Why not give it a shot? Check out page 200 for a little DIY house blend tutorial.

---

2 cups old-fashioned (rolled) oats
½ cup chopped pecans
½ cup shredded unsweetened
   coconut
2 tablespoons coconut oil, melted
2 tablespoons maple syrup

2 tablespoons cane sugar
1½ teaspoons grated fresh ginger
½ teaspoon kosher salt
¼ teaspoon ground cinnamon
½ cup pumpkin seeds
½ cup chopped dried apples

---

1. Adjust an oven rack to the middle position and preheat the oven to 325°F. Line a rimmed sheet pan with parchment paper.

2. Toss the oats, pecans, shredded coconut, and coconut oil in a large bowl, making sure everything gets nicely coated with the oil. Spread the oat mixture evenly on the prepared sheet pan (don't clean the bowl— you'll use it again in Step 3). Toast in the oven until lightly golden, 6 to 8 minutes.

3. Whisk the maple syrup, sugar, ginger, salt, and cinnamon in the bowl you used for the oats. Add the pumpkin seeds and apples and toss to combine.

4. Remove the oat mixture from the oven. Use the parchment to carefully lift and transfer the oat mixture to the maple mixture. Stir to combine, then return the parchment to the pan and spread the granola on top. Continue to bake until golden brown but not too dark, 10 to 12 minutes. Cool completely. The granola will keep in an airtight container at room temperature for up to 2 weeks.

Pumpkin Seed–
Apple Granola,
page 197

# THAI PEANUT GRANOLA

VO GF *MAKES 4 CUPS*

**W**hen I was the food editor at the digital food magazine *Tasting Table*, in a fit of inspiration, I decided to dehydrate Thai green curry paste to use as a spice seasoning in salad dressing. Cooking the spice paste at a low temperature concentrated its flavor by eliminating the moisture. Once the paste was dry and leathery, I pulverized it in a spice grinder. I love sweet-salty-spicy flavor combinations, so I decided to try the idea in granola. With the salted peanuts, tart lime, crunchy sesame seeds, and sweetness of apricot, this granola is as addictive as salty popcorn. For a delicious breakfast, try it with yogurt or milk and fresh fruit.

---

2 tablespoons Thai green curry paste, store-bought
2 cups old-fashioned (rolled) oats
1 cup roasted, salted peanuts
2 tablespoons coconut oil, melted
2 tablespoons honey

2 tablespoons cane sugar or demerara sugar
Zest of 1 lime
1 teaspoon ground coriander
½ teaspoon kosher salt
1 cup chopped dried apricots
⅓ cup sesame seeds

---

1. Adjust an oven rack to the middle position and preheat the oven to 225°F.

2. Line a rimmed sheet pan with parchment paper or a silicone baking mat and spread the curry paste on top in a fairly even, thin layer. Place the pan in the oven and dehydrate the paste until it feels dry on the surface, 25 to 35 minutes (depending on how thin the layer is). Remove from the oven and set it aside to cool for 20 minutes before scraping the paste off the parchment or baking mat with a spatula. (It should peel up pretty easily.) Transfer the dehydrated paste to a spice grinder or mortar and pestle and process as finely as possible. Increase the oven temperature to 325°F.

3. Toss together the oats, peanuts, and coconut oil in a large bowl, making sure the oats and nuts get coated evenly with the oil. Line the sheet pan with parchment paper and transfer the oat mixture to it, spreading it evenly. (Don't clean the bowl—you'll use it again in Step 4.)

# Follow Your Granola Unicorn

Don't like dried apricots? Peanuts? Ginger? Leave it out and create your own blend. What a great gift it makes—whether for a friend, new neighbor, bake sale, teacher appreciation day, or simply a self-care moment. Feel free to mix and match!

**NUTS:** Almonds, cashews, peanuts, pecans, pistachios, walnuts (or skip the nuts and double the seeds)

**FAT:** Butter, coconut oil, olive oil, pistachio oil, pumpkin seed oil, sunflower oil

**SWEETENER:** Brown sugar, cane sugar, date syrup, honey, maple sugar/syrup, pomegranate molasses

**SPICES:** Caraway, cardamom, cinnamon, cloves, coriander, ginger, nutmeg

**SEEDS:** Aniseed, chia, coriander seed, fennel, hemp, poppy, pumpkin, sesame, sunflower

**DRIED FRUITS:** Apples, apricots, blueberries, cherries, chopped mango, coconut, cranberries, currants, dates, figs, pineapple, raisins

Toast in the oven until lightly golden, 6 to 8 minutes.

4. Whisk the honey, sugar, lime zest, coriander, and salt in the bowl you used for the oats. Add the apricots and sesame seeds and stir to combine.

5. Remove the oat mixture from the oven. Use the parchment to carefully lift and transfer it to the honey mixture. Stir to combine, then return the parchment to the pan, and spread the granola on top in an even layer. Continue to bake, stirring midway through cooking, until golden brown, 20 to 25 minutes. Cool completely. The granola will keep in an airtight container for up to 2 weeks.

# CHOCOLATE BROWNIE SCONES

*MAKES 8 SCONES*

**H**ere's a fantastic excuse to eat a brownie for breakfast! Just put it in a breakfast-y package, like these rich and tender scones. Note that the scones are very dark and brown, so if you have a dark-surfaced sheet pan (which tends to cook the bottom of baked goods more), you may need to stack 2 pans together to create a layer of insulation—this will prevent the scones from burning on the bottom before they cook through.

---

1¾ cups all-purpose flour
½ cup Dutch process cocoa powder
¼ cup packed light brown sugar
1 tablespoon baking powder
½ teaspoon baking soda
¾ teaspoon kosher salt
½ cup (1 stick) cold unsalted butter, cut into very small pieces

¾ cup mini semisweet chocolate chips
1¼ cups sour cream
½ cup coarse sugar, such as turbinado or demerara
2 tablespoons unsalted butter, melted
Jam, for serving (optional)

---

1. Combine the flour, cocoa powder, light brown sugar, baking powder, baking soda, and salt in a food processor and pulse to incorporate.

2. Add the cold butter and pulse until the butter starts to become incorporated but isn't too fine, about four (1-second) pulses. Add the chocolate chips and continue to pulse until you don't see any butter pieces larger than a small pea, about four more (1-second) pulses. Add the sour cream and pulse until a tacky dough forms, four or five (1-second) pulses.

3. Line a rimmed sheet pan with parchment paper or a silicone baking mat. Spread the coarse sugar on your work surface and turn the dough out onto it. Turn the dough over so both sides are sugared, then gently press the dough into a flat rectangle, roughly 5 inches wide, 10 inches long, and ¾ inch thick. With a knife, cut the dough in half horizontally and then vertically 4 times to yield 8 equal-size pieces. Arrange the scones on the prepared pan about 1 inch apart and place them in the freezer for 45 minutes.

## Turning Breakfast into Dessert

With leftover scones or biscuits or muffins you can make some wonderful desserts. Here are some ideas to repurpose your sweet morning nibble into a delicious after-dinner treat.

- Break the pastry into small pieces and layer with whipped cream and fruit for a trifle or a shortcake.

- Halve the pastry, warm under the broiler, top with ricotta cheese and a drizzle of honey.

- Halve the pastry, slather it with butter, dip it in sugar, and caramelize it facedown in a hot pan, then serve with ice cream.

- Cut the pastry into bite-size pieces and toast in the oven; serve with skewers and dulce de leche (homemade, page 229, or store-bought) or warm chocolate ganache for dunking (like fondue; works best with scones and biscuits—muffins are too tender).

4. Adjust an oven rack to the middle position and preheat the oven to 400°F. Brush the scones with the meled butter and bake until they are firm to the touch, 20 to 24 minutes. Cool for 5 minutes, then transfer to a wire rack to cool for 1 hour. Serve warm or at room temperature (I like them with a dollop of jam on top). The scones will keep in an airtight container for 1 day.

# VEGAN (SAY WHAT?) BISCUITS

V · *MAKES 8 BISCUITS*

I'm a sucker for a tender, flaky biscuit. And, I mean really, who isn't? I used to think you needed butter and cream (or buttermilk or sour cream) for flakiness but, it turns out, fat is fat and dairy fat does not need to play a part in a great, fluffy, flaky, and flavorful biscuit. Don't believe me? Make these now! They'll blow your mind (and the mind of every vegan—and non-vegan—you know). They're even incredible turned into tomorrow's breakfast or lunch sandwich (and they re-warm beautifully in a 250°F oven).

I made these with unbleached all-purpose flour from King Arthur Flour, and I strongly recommend it for the best results. You can find it at many supermarkets as well as online at kingarthurflour.com.

---

½ cup silken tofu
½ cup almond, coconut, or soy milk
1¾ cups all-purpose flour (such as King Arthur), plus extra for shaping
2 teaspoons sugar

2 teaspoons baking powder
½ teaspoon baking soda
1 teaspoon kosher salt
4 tablespoons solid coconut oil
4 tablespoons vegan butter, such as Earth's Balance

---

1. Adjust an oven rack to the middle position and preheat the oven to 375°F. Line a rimmed sheet pan with parchment paper or a silicone baking mat.

2. Combine the tofu and almond milk in a large bowl and, with an immersion blender, puree until completely smooth. (You can also do this in a traditional blender.) Set aside.

3. Whisk the flour, sugar, baking powder, baking soda, and salt in a large bowl. Add the coconut oil and vegan butter and, with your fingers, work the fats into the flour, pressing it between your fingertips, mixing, and fluffing the flour until there aren't any butter pieces larger than a small pea.

4. Add the tofu mixture and combine with a fork until it gets too hard to stir, then, with your hand, turn and

mix the ingredients together until no dry pockets of flour remain. Heavily flour your work surface and place the dough on top. Pat the dough into a rectangle about 5 inches wide, 11 inches long, and 1-inch thick, then fold it into thirds like a business letter. Pat it out again and fold it into thirds again. Pat it out one last time (re-flouring under the dough if needed), this time into a 4 x 9-inch rectangle that's about 1½ inches thick. Slice horizontally through the middle of the rectangle and then vertically into quarters to create 8 biscuits. Place the biscuits on the prepared baking sheet, about 1 inch apart.

5. Bake the biscuits until they are golden brown, 20 to 25 minutes. Remove from the oven and serve warm or at room temperature. They will keep, in an airtight container at room temperature for up to 3 days.

## Disco Biscuits

You know disco fries (essentially fries with gravy)? Well, I hereby propose disco biscuits! Simply pair the biscuits here with the Cashew-Mushroom Gravy on page 205. The result will make any gravy-loving vegetarian or vegan glow with glee—and, yes, maybe even do a little line dance hustle to celebrate.

# VEGAN POUTINE

(V) (GF) SERVES 4

**F**rench fries. Gravy. Cheese curds. That is poutine, the wonderful assembly of decadence that warms the hearts of Québécois at greasy spoons and diners in Canada—as well as in Los Angeles, New York, and other expat outposts where you can find this heavy yet soul-satisfying dish. Here, I roast potato wedges on a sheet pan with some peppers for an effect that reminds me of country fries, then pair them with a mushroom gravy made from roasted mushrooms, cashews, and sage. It's hearty and decadent and makes a perfect breakfast, breakfast for dinner, or late-night snack.

## FOR THE CASHEW-MUSHROOM GRAVY

2 cups raw cashews

8 ounces white mushrooms, stemmed, caps thinly sliced

2 tablespoons extra-virgin olive oil

1½ teaspoons kosher salt

¼ cup fresh sage leaves, roughly chopped

1 garlic clove, roughly chopped

½ teaspoon freshly ground black pepper

## FOR THE POUTINE

1¾ pounds Yukon Gold potatoes, halved lengthwise, each half sliced into ½-inch wedges

3 tablespoons extra-virgin olive oil

1½ teaspoons kosher salt

1 medium-size red bell pepper, stemmed, seeded, and finely chopped

¼ cup finely chopped fresh chives

1. To make the cashew-mushroom gravy: Adjust an oven rack to the middle position, place a rimmed sheet pan on top, and preheat the oven to 400°F. Put the cashews in a medium-size bowl and cover with 1¼ cups water. Set aside.

2. Put the mushrooms on the hot sheet pan and toss with the olive oil and ½ teaspoon salt. Roast in the oven, stirring midway through cooking, until browned, 15 to 18 minutes. Transfer the mushrooms to a blender. Return the sheet pan to the oven and increase the oven temperature to 450°F.

3. To make the poutine: Place the potatoes, olive oil, and salt in a large bowl and toss to combine. Turn the potatoes out onto the heated sheet pan and return to the oven to roast for 15 minutes. Carefully add the red bell pepper to the potatoes, stir to incorporate, and continue to

cook until the potatoes are crisp and browned, 10 to 15 minutes more.

4. Transfer the soaked cashews and their soaking liquid to the blender with the mushrooms. Add the remaining teaspoon salt, the sage, garlic, and pepper and blend at medium-high speed until the sauce is thick, creamy, and smooth, about 1 minute.

5. Divide the potatoes among 4 plates and spoon the sauce over each serving. Sprinkle with chives and serve.

## Cashew Cream: Your New Favorite Ingredient

Infinitely variable, cashew cream is a very simple sauce to make—just soak raw cashews with water (anywhere from 30 minutes to overnight) and blend the cashews with all or some of their soaking liquid plus some garlic, salt, and pepper (the more liquid you add, the thinner the cream—feel free to experiment to determine what you like best). Add herbs of your choice for a bolder flavor.

I adore cashew cream as a protein-rich, dairy-free dressing for grain bowls and roasted veggies. It's also excellent used as gravy with biscuits (Disco Biscuits, page 204) or over oven-fried potatoes, like in the poutine here. You can even use it as a substitute for heavy cream or sour cream in cakes, muffins, and scones (page 201)—just leave out the herbs and garlic, please!

Chapter 8

# DESSERTS

Sheet pans are a natural fit for baking sweets such as shortbread, cookies, and rustic fruit tarts. They are also a great tool for simple cakes and slab pies (think regular pie baked like a giant bar cookie!). These are desserts built for pleasing a crowd. Need one cake to serve 16 and bar cookies for 20? No problem. In one fell swoop you can satisfy your obligation to the bake sale, potluck, or party—or just dessert for a Tuesday night.

# Sheet Pan Desserts—READ ME!

Here are a few considerations when baking sheet pan desserts. Read this before beginning so you can pull off any dessert in this chapter without a second thought.

**SHEET PAN SIZES FOR BAKING:** Sheet pans come in multiple sizes (see page xi)—for desserts, unless I'm baking cookies on a standard 13 x 18-inch half sheet pan, I'm using a jelly roll pan that is about 10 x 15 inches. Jelly roll pans come in many sizes but, typically, they are larger than a quarter sheet pan and smaller than a half sheet. If you end up having a little bit extra after filling your sheet pan, you can bake the excess in a ramekin or two on the side (or make a mini pie or two on the side!). A quarter sheet pan is always great for toasting coconut and nuts, or making shortbread (page 220).

**PANS WITH DARK BOTTOMS:** Whether your sheet pan is a dark-coated nonstick or a standard pan that has taken on a dark patina over time, pay attention to the bottom of your baked goods. Just like wearing black in the summer makes you hotter because the color absorbs more heat, a dark pan could potentially burn or over-brown the bottom of your cookies, tart, or slab pie before the rest of the dessert is properly baked through. To combat this effect, start the bake time as instructed and then, after 10 minutes or so (once the item has had time to start to brown), place a second sheet pan directly under the first pan to insulate it. If you don't have a second sheet pan large enough to hold the first, try elevating the pan on top of an upside-down muffin tin or an ovensafe and steady skillet.

**LINING A SHEET PAN:** We have all been there—you bake something delicious and then have to try to chisel it off the pan. With a little forethought, your cakes, bar cookies, and tarts will effortlessly lift off the surface without any sign of a struggle. I suggest you invest in a silicone baking mat. You will not be disappointed as these nonstick mats can be used over and over for sweet or savory applications, and they last for *years*. It's also a good idea to keep parchment paper (NOT waxed paper!) on hand. The sheets can often be reused. Aluminum foil is always a solid option as well.

# CHOCOLATE CHIP COOKIE CAKE WITH QUICKEST CHOCOLATE BUTTERCREAM FROSTING

*MAKES ABOUT 10 PIECES*

Take chocolate chip cookie dough, turn it into a simple cake batter with some heavy cream and an extra egg, bake it in a sheet pan, layer it with a quick and silky chocolate buttercream, and what do you have? Oh, I don't know. . . . How about bliss? You can also lose the buttercream and just serve the cake cut into squares like a tea cake, or leave the cake in a single layer and frost the top for a frosted sheet cake.

---

**FOR THE CAKE**

1 cup (2 sticks) plus 1 tablespoon unsalted butter, at room temperature
2 cups all-purpose flour
1 teaspoon baking powder
½ teaspoon kosher salt
1¼ cups packed light brown sugar
⅓ cup sugar
3 large eggs
¾ cup heavy (whipping) cream

2 teaspoons pure vanilla extract
2 cups semisweet chocolate chips

**FOR THE FROSTING**

3 sticks plus 6 tablespoons unsalted butter, at room temperature
3 cups confectioners' sugar
12 ounces semisweet chocolate, melted and cooled to room temperature (but still pourable)
1 tablespoon pure vanilla extract

---

1. To make the cake: Adjust an oven rack to the middle position and preheat the oven to 350°F. Grease the bottom and sides of a 10 x 16-inch rimmed sheet pan with 1 tablespoon butter. Line the pan with a sheet of parchment paper or aluminum foil,

pressing it into place, then flip the paper or foil, and press it into the pan so both sides are greased.

2. Whisk the flour, baking powder, and salt in a medium-size bowl and set aside.

3. Place the remaining 1 cup butter, brown sugar, and sugar in the bowl of a stand mixer (or a large bowl if using a handheld mixer) and cream together at medium speed until well combined, about 30 seconds. Increase the mixer speed to medium-high and beat until light and airy, 2 minutes. Reduce the speed to medium-low and add the eggs, one at a time, beating well after each addition and stopping to scrape the bottom and side of the bowl as needed, about 1 minute total.

4. Reduce the mixer speed to low. Add one-third of the flour mixture and, once it is mostly incorporated, add half of the heavy cream and the vanilla. Beat until nearly combined. Beat in half of the remaining flour mixture, and the remaining cream, and beat until nearly combined. Beat in the remaining flour mixture, mixing until only a few dry streaks remain, stopping the mixer to scrape the bottom and side of the bowl as needed. Add the chocolate chips and increase the mixer speed to medium-high for 20 seconds to combine.

5. With a rubber spatula, scrape the batter evenly into the prepared sheet pan. Bake until a cake tester inserted into the center of the cake comes out clean and the cake resists light pressure, 20 to 25 minutes. Remove the cake from the oven and set aside to cool completely in the pan. Invert the cake out of the pan and onto a large cutting board. Discard the parchment paper.

6. To make the frosting: Place the butter in a medium-size bowl and, with a rubber spatula, smash it and stir it. With a whisk (or handheld mixer or stand mixer), whip it slightly until it is soft and lump free. Sift the confectioners' sugar into the butter. With the spatula, stir in the sugar, then switch back to the whisk to whip it lightly. Pour in the melted chocolate and add the vanilla, whisking to combine.

7. Slice the cake in half crosswise. Add a dollop of buttercream frosting to the center of a cake plate or platter and place one cake half on top. (This helps it stick to the base.) Top the cake with one-third of the buttercream, spreading it into an even layer. Place the second cake half on top. (If the buttercream is very warm, refrigerate the first layer for 10 to 20 minutes before proceeding.) Frost the top and sides of the cake with the remaining buttercream. Refrigerate for at least 30 minutes, or for up to 2 days, before serving. (Let the cake sit out at room temperature for 20 minutes before slicing and serving.) Cover and refrigerate any leftovers, which will keep for up to 5 days.

# HONEY-GLAZED SPICE CAKE

*MAKES ABOUT 12 PIECES*

Warm and cozy. That's the feeling this cake offers. It's a great bring-along cake for a buffet or potluck, since it feeds a crowd and keeps great at room temperature. The honey glaze seals the moisture in, making this cake a keeper for days upon days. You can substitute any liqueur in place of brandy, from Grand Marnier to bourbon or spiced rum—or cut the alcohol completely and use apple cider or ginger beer instead.

### FOR THE CAKE
¾ cup (1½ sticks) unsalted butter, melted, plus 1 tablespoon unsalted butter, at room temperature
¾ cup golden raisins
¼ cup warm brandy (or apple cider)
½ cup old-fashioned (rolled) oats
2 cups all-purpose flour
1½ teaspoons baking powder
1½ teaspoons ground ginger
½ teaspoon ground allspice
½ teaspoon ground cinnamon
½ teaspoon baking soda
½ teaspoon kosher salt
¼ teaspoon ground cardamom
¼ teaspoon freshly ground black pepper
½ cup strong-brewed coffee, cooled
½ cup honey
2 teaspoons pure vanilla extract
¾ cup packed light brown sugar
2 large eggs

### FOR THE HONEY GLAZE
¼ cup honey
2 to 2½ cups confectioners' sugar

1. Adjust an oven rack to the middle position and preheat the oven to 350°F. Grease a 10 x 16-inch rimmed sheet pan with 1 tablespoon room-temperature butter, then line with a sheet of parchment paper or aluminum foil (you may need 2 sheets), pressing it into the corners and up the sides so the entire pan is covered. Flip the paper or foil so both sides are greased, and press it back into the pan and up and over the sides.

2. To make the cake: Place the raisins in the bowl of a food processor and pulse until they are broken into small pieces. Pour the warm brandy into a small bowl, add the raisins, cover with plastic wrap, and set aside.

3. Place the oats in a spice grinder (or the food processor, removing and

cleaning the blade and wiping the bowl dry first) and process until finely ground. Transfer the oats to a medium-size bowl and whisk in the flour, baking powder, ginger, allspice, cinnamon, baking soda, salt, cardamom, and pepper. Whisk the coffee, honey, and vanilla in a liquid measuring cup.

4. Vigorously whisk the brown sugar and eggs in a large bowl until pale and creamy, 1 to 2 minutes. Whisk in the coffee mixture, then whisk in the melted butter. Add the oat mixture and stir with a wooden spoon to combine. With a slotted spoon, add the raisins to the batter, stirring to incorporate. (Reserve the brandy for the glaze.)

5. With a rubber spatula, scrape the batter into the prepared sheet pan, spreading it evenly, and bake until a cake tester inserted into the center comes out clean, about 15 minutes.

6. While the cake bakes, make the glaze: Place the honey in a medium-size bowl. Transfer the reserved brandy to a measuring cup and add enough hot water to make ¼ cup. Pour the liquid over the honey and whisk to combine. Whisk in 2 cups confectioners' sugar until smooth. (The glaze will be thin—if it looks too watery, add the remaining ½ cup confectioners' sugar.)

7. Let the cake cool in the pan for 15 minutes, then use the aluminum foil to carefully lift it from the pan and set it on a wire rack. With a teaspoon or pastry brush, drizzle the glaze over the surface of the still-warm cake. Set aside to cool completely, slice, and serve. (You can also cool the cake completely, then slice it and glaze it so the glaze drips down the sides of each square.) The cake will keep in an airtight container (or in the sheet pan covered with plastic wrap) at room temperature for up to 5 days.

# PLUM CAKE WITH WALNUT STREUSEL

*MAKES ABOUT 12 PIECES*

This is, hands-down, my favorite coffee cake, like, ever. I love how plums, when they're baked into batter, soften and leach their gorgeous purple color (either from the skin, flesh, or both) right into the crumb. Sweet-tart, they add moisture and variation to this tasty, tender slab cake. The streusel is crumbly and buttery and, to me, perfect. If you're not into walnuts, use any nut you like. You can also make the cake with raspberries, blueberries, apricots, blackberries, or ripe pears.

---

1 tablespoon unsalted butter, at room temperature

**FOR THE WALNUT STREUSEL**
1 cup finely chopped walnuts
1 cup all-purpose flour
¾ cup packed light brown sugar
¼ cup sugar
½ teaspoon kosher salt
½ cup (1 stick) cold unsalted butter, cut into very small pieces

**FOR THE PLUM CAKE**
2½ cups all-purpose flour
1 teaspoon baking powder
½ teaspoon kosher salt
¼ teaspoon baking soda
3 large eggs
¾ cup sugar
2 teaspoons pure vanilla extract
1 cup sour cream
1 cup (2 sticks) unsalted butter, melted
4 plums or pluots, halved, pitted, and roughly chopped (about 1½ cups)

---

1. Adjust an oven rack to the middle position and preheat the oven to 350°F. Grease the bottom of a 10 x 16-inch rimmed sheet pan with 1 tablespoon room-temperature butter. Line the pan with parchment paper (you may need 2 sheets) so the bottom and sides are covered and there is enough paper sticking above the rim to help remove the cake from the pan for serving. Press the paper into the pan, then flip it, so both sides are greased, and press it back into the pan. Set aside.

2. To make the streusel: Combine the walnuts, flour, brown sugar, sugar, and salt in a medium-size bowl. Add the butter and, with your fingers, work it in until the mixture is very fine and crumbly and no butter pieces larger than a small pea remain. Set aside.

**3.** To make the cake: Whisk the flour, baking powder, salt, and baking soda in a medium-size bowl. Whisk the eggs, sugar, and vanilla in a large bowl until foamy and creamy, about 2 minutes (or use an electric mixer if you like). Whisk in the sour cream, then add the flour mixture, whisking until just a streak or two of dry ingredients remains. Pour in the melted butter and whisk until just combined.

**4.** Pour the batter into the prepared sheet pan and sprinkle the plums over the top, followed by the streusel. Bake until the cake is golden brown and resists light pressure, 25 to 30 minutes. Remove from the oven and set aside to cool completely. Use the parchment paper to help lift the cake from the pan, slice, and serve. The cake will keep in an airtight container at room temperature for 3 to 4 days.

# RUSTIC PEAR GALETTE

*SERVES 6*

Despite its fussy-sounding name, a galette is just a round of piecrust dough, with fruit in the middle, that is folded up around the fruit in pretty pleats. They are one of my favorite desserts to make because the filling can be easily changed to reflect what is in season (see page 218 for variations). Very simple and very rustic, you can easily make this with store-bought piecrust dough if you don't feel like making your own.

### FOR THE GALETTE DOUGH
1 large egg yolk
½ teaspoon pure vanilla extract
2½ cups all-purpose flour, plus extra
    for rolling the dough
3 tablespoons sugar
¼ teaspoon kosher salt
¾ cup (1½ sticks) cold unsalted
    butter, cut into ½-inch pieces
2 tablespoons cold cream cheese
4 to 6 tablespoons ice water

### FOR THE PEAR FILLING
3 medium-ripe Bartlett or Anjou
    pears, cored and cut into ¼-inch-
    thick slices
Finely grated zest of 1 lemon
1 tablespoon fresh lemon juice
⅓ cup sugar, plus 1 tablespoon for
    sprinkling
½ teaspoon ground cinnamon
¼ teaspoon ground cardamom
    (optional)
⅛ teaspoon plus a pinch of kosher
    salt
1 large egg
1 tablespoon unsalted butter

1. To make the galette dough: Whisk the egg yolk and vanilla in a small bowl and set aside. Combine the flour, sugar, and salt in the bowl of a food processor and pulse to combine (or place in a large bowl if making the dough by hand). Add the butter and pulse 3 times (or work it in for about 10 seconds by hand, rubbing the butter into the flour with your fingertips). Add the cream cheese and pulse until the mixture looks like cornmeal, about eight (1-second) pulses (or use your fingers to rub the cream cheese and butter into the flour). Add the egg mixture and pulse to combine (or use a fork to stir it in). Transfer the mixture to a large bowl and, with a fork, stir in 4 tablespoons of the ice water. Squeeze the dough together—if it holds its shape, there's no need to add more water. If it is dry, add 1 to 2 tablespoons more of the remaining ice water, stir, and make sure the dough holds together before proceeding.

2. Set a large sheet of plastic wrap onto your work surface. Gather the dough into a ball and press it onto the plastic into a ½-inch-thick circle. Wrap completely with the plastic wrap, and refrigerate until chilled, at least 1 hour or up to 3 days.

3. To make the pear filling: Line a rimmed sheet pan with parchment paper or a silicone baking mat. Place the pears in a medium-size bowl and toss with the lemon zest and juice, ⅓ cup sugar, cinnamon, cardamom (if using), and salt. Set aside.

## A Galette for Any Season

A galette is a great go-to dessert any time of year. Pears are a beautiful option for fall and winter; however lots of fruits fit the bill when pears aren't in season (or if you just feel like switching it up). Substitute about 1¼ pounds of fruit for the pears, depending on what is at its peak—and feel free to combine fruits as you like.

**SPRING GALETTE:** Rhubarb*, strawberries**

**SUMMER GALETTE:** Apricots, blueberries**, nectarines, sour cherries*

**FALL GALETTE:** Apples, pears, plums

**WINTER GALETTE:** Apples, mangos, pears, pineapple

*Add a little extra sugar (about ¼ cup, or even a little more if using extra tart fruit like rhubarb or cranberries) when using these sweet-tart fruits.

**Toss the fruit with a little cornstarch (about 1 tablespoon) to thicken their juices if you worry the cooked fruit will be runny (like peaches, strawberries, and blueberries).

4. Whisk the egg, 1 tablespoon water, and a pinch of salt in a small bowl. Remove the dough from the refrigerator and place it on a lightly floured work surface. Lightly flour the top and let the dough warm up for 10 to 15 minutes, then roll it into a 15- to 16-inch circle about ¼ inch thick. Transfer the dough to the prepared sheet pan and pile the pears in the middle, leaving a 3-inch border around the edges. Cut the butter into small pieces and dot the top of the pears with it. Loosely fold the edges of the dough around the pears, pleating the dough as you go, leaving the tart open in the middle.

5. Brush the dough with the egg wash and sprinkle the dough with the remaining tablespoon sugar. Refrigerate the tart on the sheet pan for 30 minutes, or up to overnight (if refrigerating overnight, wrap the sheet pan in plastic wrap).

6. Adjust an oven rack to the middle position and preheat the oven to 400°F. Bake the tart until the crust is deeply golden brown, 30 to 40 minutes, then cool completely on a wire rack. Slice into pieces and serve. Leftovers will keep at room temperature for 1 day or covered in the refrigerator for up to 2 days (rewarm in the oven to crisp the dough before serving).

# CINNAMON-SUGAR PALMIERS

*MAKES ABOUT 2 DOZEN PALMIERS*

A great palmier tastes like the best piece of cinnamon-sugar toast you have ever eaten. They are made from incredibly flaky puff pastry—be sure to buy all-butter puff pastry such as Dufour, as it really makes an enormous difference in the flavor (you can find it in the freezer section of most supermarkets).

---

¼ cup sugar
1 teaspoon ground cinnamon
¼ teaspoon ground cardamom

¼ teaspoon kosher salt
1 sheet (about 12 ounces) thawed
    frozen puff pastry

---

1. Adjust an oven rack to the middle position and preheat the oven to 400°F. Line a rimmed sheet pan with parchment paper or a silicone baking mat.

2. Mix the sugar, cinnamon, cardamom, and salt together in a medium-size bowl. Place the puff pastry on your work surface and sprinkle each side with 1 tablespoon of the sugar mixture.

3. Roll out the pastry until it is twice as long as it is wide. (Generally, depending on the size of your pastry to begin with, you will be able to get it to about 16 inches long, 8 inches wide, and ⅛ inch thick.) Fold the top down to the middle and the bottom up to the middle toward an invisible centerline, so the edges kiss. Sprinkle with 1 tablespoon of the sugar mixture and gently roll the pastry again, lengthwise, to flatten it. Fold the top over the bottom so the top edge and bottom edge meet, then gently roll lengthwise again to flatten it. Thinly slice the pastry crosswise into ¼-inch-wide pieces and lay them flat on the prepared baking sheet. Sprinkle the top with the remaining sugar mixture, place another piece of parchment on top, and set a second sheet pan on top to weigh the palmiers down.

4. Bake the palmiers until they are golden brown and crisp, 22 to 26 minutes. Transfer to a wire rack to cool completely. The palmiers will keep in an airtight container at room temperature for up to 3 days (depending on the humidity of your kitchen).

# CITRUS-ALMOND SHORTBARS

*MAKES 20 BARS*

We have a tradition at home called breakfast cookies—no, they're *not* healthy granola cookies. Rather, they're sweet and yummy (and yes, a little naughty first thing in the morning) to dunk into coffee or have with hot cocoa. It's not the most virtuous habit, but it sure is fun to start the day with a little nibble of something sweet! The orange zest in these bars brightens their flavor—if you have grapefruit around, zest a little and add that, too, or try tangerine, tangelo, pomelo. . . . You don't *always* have to stick to the same old citrus go-tos, you know? Sometimes I'll even add a tablespoon of orange flower water or rose water and a pinch of cardamom for a very Moroccan vibe. These cookies last a good long while in an airtight container at room temperature, or package them in cellophane or parchment for a thoughtful gift.

---

1 tablespoon unsalted butter, at room temperature, plus 10 tablespoons (1¼ sticks) cold unsalted butter, cut into ½-inch pieces
1 cup sliced almonds
¾ cup plus 1 tablespoon granulated sugar

1 tablespoon finely grated orange zest (or grapefruit zest or tangerine zest)
1½ cups all-purpose flour
¼ cup whole-wheat pastry flour
⅓ cup confectioners' sugar, plus extra for serving
1½ teaspoons kosher salt
1 tablespoon honey

---

1. Adjust an oven rack to the middle position and preheat the oven to 450°F. Lightly coat a quarter sheet pan with the room-temperature butter and set aside.

2. Place the almonds in the bowl of a food processor and process until they are finely ground, about 8 seconds. Rub together the ¾ cup granulated sugar and orange zest in a small bowl until the sugar is very fragrant, about 10 seconds. Add the sugar to the almonds and pulse 3 times to combine.

3. Add the all-purpose flour, whole-wheat pastry flour, confectioners' sugar, and salt and pulse to combine. Uncover the machine, drizzle in the

honey, and sprinkle the cold butter pieces over the top. Cover and pulse until the mixture looks like coarse cornmeal and rides up the side of the bowl, fifteen to twenty (1-second) pulses.

4. Turn the mixture out onto the prepared sheet pan and spread it evenly. With the bottom of a measuring cup, press the dough into the corners, edges, and across the entire sheet pan to create a solid, even layer. Drag the back of a knife through the dough to score it into squares—I like to mark it in 4 columns lengthwise and 5 rows crosswise. Place the sheet pan in the oven and reduce the temperature to 300°F. Bake, rotating the pan midway through, until golden brown and fragrant, 20 to 25 minutes.

5. Cool for 10 minutes, and sprinkle with the remaining tablespoon of granulated sugar. Cool for 10 minutes more, then use a sharp knife to cut the shortbread into pieces along the score lines. Cool completely in the pan, then transfer to an airtight container and sprinkle with confectioners' sugar before serving. The bars will keep in an airtight container at room temperature for up to 1 week.

## Easy Press-In Crust Technique

For the Citrus-Almond Shortbars and the base layer crust for the Cherry Bomb Bars (page 226), the Dulce de Leche Pumpkin Pie Squares (page 228), and the Chocolate Cream Pie Bars (page 230), you have to press the crumbly dough layer into the pan evenly and neatly so it's approximately the same thickness from end to end. While the bottom of a measuring cup is great for tamping the crust down and evening it out, there is an even easier (and faster) option if you have a second same-size sheet pan. Disperse the crumbs somewhat evenly across the pan, pressing them down slightly, then place a large sheet of plastic wrap (or parchment paper) on top, and set a same-size sheet pan on top of the crust. Press down. Remove the sheet pan and the plastic or parchment and you have a perfectly pressed-in crust!

# KITCHEN SINK COOKIES

*MAKES ABOUT 2 DOZEN COOKIES*

These have become *the* Santa cookies for my boys—we put them out every Christmas Eve for Saint Nick. Their reasoning? Santa may have cookie fatigue by the time he reaches New York City, so why not give him a cookie that has it all? Chocolate chips, oats, cinnamon, coconut, dried cherries, nuts. Good call, boys—no wonder Santa treats you so well!

2¼ cups old-fashioned (rolled) oats
2 cups all-purpose flour
1¼ cups unsweetened coconut flakes
2 teaspoons ground cinnamon
1 teaspoon baking soda
1 teaspoon kosher salt
1 cup plus 2 tablespoons
    (2¼ sticks) unsalted butter,
    at room temperature
¼ cup cream cheese, at room
    temperature

¾ cup packed light brown sugar
¾ cup sugar
2 large eggs
1 tablespoon pure vanilla extract
1 cup bite-size dried fruit (apples,
    apricots, cherries, cranberries,
    dates, prunes, raisins)
1 cup semisweet chocolate chips
1 cup roughly chopped toasted
    nuts (almonds, cashews, peanuts,
    pecans, and/or walnuts)

1. Adjust an oven rack to the middle position and preheat the oven to 350°F. Line a rimmed sheet pan with parchment paper or a silicone baking mat.

2. Whisk the oats, flour, coconut, cinnamon, baking soda, and salt in a large bowl.

3. Place the butter and cream cheese in the bowl of a stand mixer (or a large bowl if using a handheld mixer) and cream together at medium speed until well combined, about 30 seconds. Add the brown sugar and sugar and continue to cream at medium-high speed until light and airy, about 2 minutes.

4. Add the eggs, one at a time, mixing on medium speed between additions until the eggs are well combined. Add the vanilla, mix to combine, then reduce the mixer speed to medium-low and add the oat mixture in thirds, beating to combine after each addition. Once only a few dry streaks remain, add the dried fruit, chocolate chips,

and nuts and mix at medium-low speed until well combined, about 30 seconds.

5. Scoop half of the dough into 12 mounds, shaping each into a round before placing it on the prepared sheet pan (about 2 inches apart). Bake until the cookies are set and golden brown around the edges, 14 to 16 minutes. Let the cookies cool and set up on the sheet pan for 5 minutes before transferring to a wire rack to cool completely. Repeat with the remaining cookie dough. The cookies will keep in an airtight container at room temperature for up to 1 week.

## Salty Sweet Delicious

Salt is a necessary component to dessert—think kettle corn and salted caramel ice cream, or chocolate-covered pretzels! It may sound counterintuitive but, without salt, the taste of a dessert falls a little flat—you may not be able to tell when salt is *in* a dessert, but I almost guarantee you'll notice it missing when it's *not* there. A pinch of salt makes fruit taste brighter, chocolate taste richer, and butter taste, well, better. I generally use kosher salt across the board, even in baked goods, because I kind of like when you get the occasional salty granule that stands out against the sweet. If that's not your jam, you could absolutely use table salt instead (just use half the amount called for in the recipe) for a more integrated flavor. Sometimes, like in the No-Bake Choco-Fudge Bars (page 232) or the Cherry Bomb Bars (page 226), I like to sprinkle flaky salt over the finished item. Just the slightest pinch is enough to make a difference. Try it—you'll be pleasantly surprised!

# CHOCOLATE-CHOCOLATE SPARKLERS

*MAKES 18 COOKIES*

Crackly on the surface from coarse sugar and chocolaty-decadent-chewy at the core, these cookies have a perfect balance of crisp edge to soft center. Their give makes them a fantastic cookie to turn into an ice cream sandwich.

---

2¼ cups all-purpose flour
1 teaspoon baking soda
½ teaspoon kosher salt
¾ cup (1½ sticks) unsalted butter,
    at room temperature
½ cup packed dark brown sugar
1 large egg yolk
1 teaspoon pure vanilla extract

¼ cup dark molasses
¼ cup light corn syrup
¼ cup (about 4 ounces)
    semisweet chocolate, melted
¾ cup semisweet chocolate chips
¾ cup coarse demerara sugar
    or turbinado sugar

---

1. Adjust an oven rack to the middle position and preheat the oven to 350°F. Line a sheet pan with parchment paper or a silicone baking mat.

2. Whisk the flour, baking soda, and salt in a medium-size bowl until well combined and set aside.

3. Place the butter in the bowl of a stand mixer fitted with the paddle attachment (or in a large bowl if using a handheld mixer). Add the brown sugar and beat at medium-high speed until airy, about 2 minutes. Reduce the speed to medium-low, add the egg yolk and vanilla, increase the speed to medium-high, and beat until combined, about 15 seconds. Turn off the mixer and scrape down the side and bottom of the bowl as needed. With the mixer on medium-low, add the molasses, corn syrup, and melted chocolate. Increase the speed to medium and beat until well combined, about 20 seconds.

4. Stop the mixer and add the flour mixture. Mix at low speed until almost no dry streaks remain. Add the chocolate chips and keep mixing at low speed until well combined, about 30 seconds total. Scrape the bottom and side of the bowl.

5. Place the demerara sugar in a medium-size bowl. With a large spoon, scoop about 2 tablespoons of dough from the bowl and use another spoon to scrape it into the sugar, rolling it around a bit to coat the top of the cookie. (The dough will be soft—you can wet your hands with a little ice water to prevent sticking, but it's best just to handle it gently.) Place the cookie on the prepared sheet pan. Repeat, spacing the cookies 1½ inches apart (you will need to bake in two batches; if you want to bake them all at once, prepare 2 sheet pans as instructed in Step 1, and bake them on the upper-middle and lower-middle racks, switching the pans to the different racks midway through baking).

6. Bake until the edges are set but the cookies seem soft in the center (like they could use another minute in the oven), about 11 minutes. Remove the sheet pan from the oven, give it a bang on the counter, and let the cookies sit for 5 minutes before transferring them with a spatula to a wire rack to cool completely. Repeat (if necessary) with the remaining dough. The cookies will keep in an airtight container at room temperature for up to 1 week. (Alternatively, you can shape the remaining dough into balls, freeze them, dip them in water and roll them in sugar, transfer to a gallon-size resealable freezer bag, and keep frozen to bake another time.)

## Cookies Now and Later

I often bake a half dozen cookies for now . . . and then freeze the rest of the dough in balls to bake as I like (impromptu hostess gift; dessert bring-along to a dinner party; midweek treat just because). To do this, portion the cookie dough into balls and place them on a baking sheet or even a large plate. Freeze until they are hard—about 2 hours—then transfer to a resealable freezer bag. Label the bag so you know what kind of cookies you have and how long to bake them (the cookies may need a minute or two longer to bake up), and you're all set!

For cookies that call for a sugar coating, like the Chocolate-Chocolate Sparklers, I skip the sugaring until the dough balls are frozen, then dip them in water before rolling the tops in sugar (when they're frozen, the sugar won't stick to the dough unless the sugar has something to adhere to).

# CHERRY BOMB BARS

*MAKES 20 BARS*

For these bars, you take part of their cookie base and fluff it out to create a streusel topping—so efficient! The jammy center is made with pureed Luxardo cherries, also known as the original maraschino cherries (not those insanely sweet cherries you grew up with in your kiddie cocktail; you can buy them at gourmet markets and online). Sometimes I sprinkle a little *fleur de sel* or Maldon sea salt over the top of the bars just because I love how the salt plays off the buttery sweetness of the cookie layers.

---

1 cup plus 2 tablespoons (2¼ sticks) cold, unsalted butter, cut into ½-inch pieces, plus 6 tablespoons unsalted butter, at room temperature

1 jar (14 ounces) Luxardo maraschino cherries

1 cup cherry jam or preserves (strawberry, plum, or seedless raspberry all work, too)

1¾ cups whole-wheat pastry flour

1½ cups all-purpose flour

⅔ cup almond meal

¾ cup confectioners' sugar, plus extra for serving

⅓ cup packed light brown sugar

¾ teaspoon baking soda

1½ teaspoons kosher salt

---

1. Adjust an oven rack to the middle position and preheat the oven to 350°F. Grease a 10 x 16-inch rimmed sheet pan with 1 tablespoon room-temperature butter and set aside.

2. Combine the cherries and their liquid with the jam in a food processor or blender and process until mostly smooth. Transfer to a medium-size bowl and set aside.

3. Combine the pastry flour, all-purpose flour, almond meal, confectioners' sugar, brown sugar, baking soda, and salt in the clean bowl of a food processor and pulse 4 or 5 times to mix. Add the cold butter and pulse until there are no pieces larger than a lentil, about ten (1-second) pulses. Measure 4 cups of the flour mixture into the prepared sheet pan and, with the bottom of a measuring cup, press it to the edges of the pan in an even layer. (Don't worry about working the crust up the sides of the pan.)

4. Transfer the remaining flour mixture to a medium-size bowl. Add the remaining 5 tablespoons room-temperature butter and, with your

fingers, work it in to create a chunky, streusel-like mixture.

5. With a butter knife or an offset spatula, spread the cherry puree evenly over the crust. Sprinkle with the streusel topping.

6. Bake, turning the pan midway through baking, until the topping is golden brown, about 30 minutes. Cool completely before slicing into 20 bars. The bars will keep in an airtight container at room temperature for up to 1 week.

# DULCE DE LECHE PUMPKIN PIE SQUARES

*MAKES 28 BARS*

Traditions are nice, but it can also be really fun to break them. One Thanksgiving, I had family in town from out of the country and I made the wackiest feast—grilled turkey with Korean barbecue sauce, roasted sweet potatoes with Indian spices, and these fantastic Dulce de Leche Pumpkin Pie Squares—they have a delicious graham cracker crust and a dense, sweet, pumpkin-y filling. The dulce de leche caramel adds an extra dimension of complexity and decadence.

---

½ cup (1 stick) unsalted butter, melted, plus 1 tablespoon unsalted butter, at room temperature
1 box (14.4 ounces) graham crackers
¾ teaspoon kosher salt
1½ cups packed dark brown sugar
1 tablespoon ground cinnamon
1 tablespoon ground ginger
¼ teaspoon freshly grated nutmeg
¼ teaspoon ground cloves

1 can (15 ounces) pumpkin puree (not canned pumpkin pie mix)
1⅓ cups buttermilk
4 large eggs
1½ cups (about 14 ounces) dulce de leche, homemade (see box) or store-bought
Lightly Sweetened Whipped Cream (recipe follows), for serving

---

1. Adjust an oven rack to the middle position and preheat the oven to 350°F. Grease a 10 x 16-inch rimmed baking sheet with the tablespoon of room-temperature butter and set aside.

2. Place the graham crackers in the bowl of a food processor and process into fine crumbs. Add ¼ teaspoon salt, pulse 2 times, and add the melted butter. Pulse until the mixture is well combined and holds together when pressed, about eight (1-second) pulses. Turn the crumbs out onto the prepared baking sheet and, with the bottom of a measuring cup, press them to the edges of the pan in a solid even layer. (Don't worry about working the crumbs up the sides of the pan.) Bake the crust until it feels firm and somewhat dry on the surface, about 8 minutes.

3. Wipe out the food processor with a damp paper towel. To the processor, add the brown sugar, cinnamon, ginger, nutmeg, cloves,

and remaining ½ teaspoon salt and process until smooth. Add the pumpkin, buttermilk, and eggs and process until well combined.

4. With a butter knife or an offset spatula, evenly spread the dulce de leche over the crust. Pour the pumpkin filling over the top, shaking the pan to disperse it evenly.

5. Bake the squares until the center jiggles only slightly when tapped, about 30 minutes. Cool completely before slicing crosswise into 28 bars. Serve with a dollop of whipped cream. The bars will keep in an airtight container in the refrigerator for up to 3 days (the crust will become softer the longer the bars are stored in the fridge).

## "Homemade" Dulce de Leche

It's incredibly easy to make your own dulce de leche. Simply peel the label from an unopened 14-ounce can of sweetened condensed milk and place the can in a pot of simmering water. Make sure the can is completely covered by water to a depth of 1 to 2 inches. Gently simmer for 2 hours—checking occasionally to make sure the can is still submerged and adding water if needed. Use tongs to flip the can and simmer for 1½ hours more. Remove the can from the water and set aside to cool completely before opening and using.

**NOTE:** Buy the cans of sweetened condensed milk that *do not* have the peel-away lid—apparently these can explode during cooking (though it has never—thankfully—happened to me!).

# LIGHTLY SWEETENED WHIPPED CREAM

GF *MAKES ABOUT 2 CUPS*

1 cup heavy (whipping) cream
1 teaspoon pure vanilla extract

3 tablespoons sugar

Combine the cream, vanilla, and sugar in the bowl of a stand mixer fitted with the whisk attachment (or in a large bowl if using a handheld mixer or a balloon whisk) and whip until the cream holds medium-size peaks. Serve immediately or cover the bowl with plastic wrap and refrigerate for up to 1 day (whisk again to fluff before serving).

# CHOCOLATE CREAM PIE SQUARES

*MAKES 20 BARS*

**M**arch 14 is Pie Day (you know, because pi is 3.14 . . . ) and, one year, my boys and I decided to go find us some pie to celebrate. Every pie shop we could think of in Brooklyn *and* Manhattan had a line out the door, so we beelined it straight to the grocery store to buy our own pie fixings, thank you very much. I made a very simple chocolate cream pie that was so rich and soulful, we decided every Pie Day would be Chocolate Cream Pie Day from that point forward. Made in a sheet pan, this is simply chocolate cream pie . . . squared.

---

7 tablespoons unsalted butter, melted, plus 2 tablespoons unsalted butter, at room temperature

1 package (14.3 ounces) Oreo cookies (about 38 Oreos)

8 ounces semisweet chocolate, finely chopped, or chocolate chips

2½ cups heavy (whipping) cream

¼ cup confectioners' sugar

1 teaspoon pure vanilla extract

---

1. Adjust an oven rack to the middle position and preheat the oven to 350°F. Grease a 10 x 16-inch rimmed sheet pan with 1 tablespoon room-temperature butter and set aside.

2. Place the Oreos in the bowl of a food processor and pulverize until fine. Add the melted butter and continue to process until the crumbs hold together when squeezed, about five (1-second) pulses. Turn the cookie crumbs out onto the prepared sheet pan and, with the bottom of a measuring cup, press them to the edges of the prepared pan in an even layer. (Don't worry about working the crumbs up the sides of the pan.) Bake the crust until it is set, about 8 minutes. Set aside to cool.

3. Add the chocolate and 1¼ cups cream to a microwave-safe bowl and microwave in 20-second increments, stirring between each, until the chocolate is completely melted, about 1½ minutes. Whisk until glossy and smooth. Whisk in the remaining tablespoon of room-temperature butter and pour the chocolate mixture over the baked crust, spreading it evenly with an offset spatula. Cover the pan with plastic wrap and refrigerate until

the filling is completely set, about 2 hours.

4. Combine the remaining 1¼ cups cream, confectioners' sugar, and vanilla in a medium-size bowl. Beat with a handheld mixer or a whisk (or using a stand mixer fitted with a whisk) at medium-high speed until the mixture forms stiff peaks. Spread the cream over the chocolate filling. Slice into 20 bars and serve. The bars will keep in an airtight container (or in the sheet pan covered with plastic wrap) in the refrigerator for up to 3 days.

# NO-BAKE CHOCO-FUDGE BARS

(V) (GF) *MAKES 24 SMALL SQUARES*

As decadent as a truffle but infinitely easier to make, these squares take, literally, minutes to put together. After a brief rest in the freezer they are ready to slice and serve, making them a great after-dinner treat. The dried cherries offer a sweet-tart base to bounce off the chocolate's richness, though dates are an excellent option as well.

---

1½ cups roasted, salted peanuts
¼ cup Dutch process cocoa
¼ teaspoon kosher salt
1¼ cups dried cherries
2 tablespoons smooth peanut butter (if needed)

8 ounces semisweet chocolate, finely chopped
⅔ cup lite coconut milk
1½ tablespoons coconut oil, melted
Flaky salt, for finishing (optional)

---

1. Combine the peanuts, cocoa powder, and salt in the bowl of a food processor and process until finely ground, about ten (1-second) pulses. Add the cherries and process until you can squeeze the mixture together without it breaking apart easily, about 6 seconds. (Add the peanut butter, if needed, to help bind it.)

2. Line a quarter sheet pan with parchment paper and turn the peanut mixture out onto the pan, spreading it into an even layer. Place a sheet of plastic wrap on top of the peanut mixture and, with the bottom of a measuring cup, press it into a solid and even layer (the plastic wrap helps prevent it from sticking to the measuring cup). Put the sheet pan in the freezer to set, 15 minutes.

3. Meanwhile, place the chocolate in a microwave-safe bowl and microwave in 20-second increments, stirring between each, until the chocolate is completely melted, about 1½ minutes. Whisk in the coconut milk and the coconut oil until smooth. Pour the chocolate mixture over the frozen base, spreading it into an even layer with a rubber spatula. Sprinkle with flaky salt (if using) and put the pan back in the freezer to set, at least 20 minutes. Cut into 24 small squares. Refrigerate until serving. The bars will keep, covered and refrigerated (or frozen), for up to 1 week. Serve cold.

# ROASTED FALL FRUIT OVER MASCARPONE CREAM

GF  *SERVES 6*

Roasting fruit in wine is a very elegant way to make dessert, not to mention to make it without breaking much of a sweat. I first learned the trick of roasting grapes in wine from a Lidia Bastianich cookbook—you know her, the grand dame of Italian cooking. I was stunned—not just by the simplicity, but also by the deliciousness of the fruit and accompanying syrup. Spooned over mascarpone lightened by whipped cream (with sugar and some liqueur to keep things interesting!), it is elegance and unfussiness at their finest. Save leftovers of fruit (if you have any) for morning oatmeal (because . . . why not?).

---

2 teaspoons grapeseed oil
2 cups halved red grapes
3 ripe pears, halved, cored, and chopped into ¾-inch pieces
2 plums, halved, pitted, and chopped into ¾-inch pieces
¼ cup sugar

¾ cup Vin Santo or white Moscato wine (see Box, page 234)
¾ cup heavy (whipping) cream
2 tablespoons Amaretto or Frangelico liqueur (optional)
½ cup confectioners' sugar
1 cup mascarpone cheese

---

1. Adjust an oven rack to the middle position and preheat the oven to 400°F. Lightly coat a rimmed sheet pan with the oil.

2. Toss the grapes, pears, and plums with the sugar in a large bowl. Turn the fruit out onto the prepared pan in an even layer and roast until it just starts to get juicy, 10 to 15 minutes. Add the wine and continue to roast until the fruit softens and shrivels a bit, 10 to 15 minutes more. Transfer to a heatproof bowl.

3. Place the heavy cream in a medium-size bowl and whisk until it forms soft peaks. Add the liqueur (if using) and confectioners' sugar and continue to whisk until it holds stiff peaks. (Alternatively, beat it at medium-high speed with a handheld mixer or stand mixer.) Whisk in the mascarpone. (The

mascarpone cream can be made up to 6 hours ahead of time; store it in an airtight container in the fridge.)

4. Divide the mascarpone cream among 6 dessert bowls. Top each serving with the fruit and syrup and serve.

# VEGAN STICKY TOFFEE PUDDING

**(V)** *SERVES 8 TO 10*

**I**f you'd like to create a pan of sunshine, pure happiness, and utter indulgence, look no further. This is sticky, sweet, and caramel-y, thanks to the hard sauce that is almost like butterscotch poured over the top (you can substitute apple cider for the rum if you like). The recipe can easily be doubled for a half sheet pan, which makes it a great choice for parties and potlucks, too. Since the dessert is vegan, I don't use eggs in it—instead I use flaxseeds as a binder (they add omega-3s and fiber, too).

---

**FOR THE PUDDING**
5 tablespoons coconut oil, melted
1¼ cups all-purpose flour
1 teaspoon baking soda
½ teaspoon kosher salt
¾ cup sugar
2 tablespoons flaxseed
10 ounces (1¾ cups) pitted dates
  (preferably Medjool)
1 cup coconut milk (don't use lite
  coconut milk)

¼ cup date syrup or maple syrup
  (see box, below)
½ cup warm water
2 teaspoons pure vanilla extract

**FOR THE HARD SAUCE**
4 tablespoons vegan butter
  (such as Earth's Balance)
½ cup coconut milk (don't use lite
  coconut milk)
½ cup packed dark brown sugar
3 tablespoons dark rum

---

1. Adjust an oven rack to the middle position and preheat the oven to 350°F. Grease a 10 x 16-inch sheet pan with 1 tablespoon coconut oil and set aside.

2. To make the pudding: Whisk the flour, baking soda, and salt in a large bowl and set aside.

3. Combine the sugar and flaxseed in the bowl of a food processor and process until the flaxseed is finely

### Dates Meet Syrup

Date syrup is a fruit syrup extracted from dates—it tastes deep and caramel-y, almost like molasses but less assertive. Also known as *silan*, it can be found in most Middle Eastern markets.

ground. Add the dates and pulse for five (1-second) bursts. Add the coconut milk and syrup and process to combine, then add the warm water and vanilla and process until smooth, about 5 seconds. With the food processor running, add the remaining coconut oil.

4. Pour the date mixture into the flour mixture and stir to combine. Pour the batter into the prepared pan and bake until the center resists light pressure, about 20 minutes. Set the pudding aside, but keep the oven on.

5. While the pudding bakes, make the sauce: Place the vegan butter and coconut milk in a microwave-safe bowl and heat until hot but not boiling, 1 to 1½ minutes. Stir in the sugar and whisk until melted, then whisk in the rum.

6. Pour the warm sauce over the pudding, encouraging it with a spoon to spread evenly over the pudding, getting into all the corners and edges. (It will pool at first but it will soak in.) Turn off the oven and let the pudding sit in the warm oven for 15 minutes. Remove from the oven and let it cool for at least 20 minutes before slicing and serving (or refrigerate for up to 5 days and reheat in a warm oven or the microwave before serving).

# CONVERSION TABLES

Please note that all conversions are approximate but close enough to be useful when converting from one system to another.

## OVEN TEMPERATURES

| FAHRENHEIT | GAS MARK | CELSIUS |
|---|---|---|
| 250 | ½ | 120 |
| 275 | 1 | 140 |
| 300 | 2 | 150 |
| 325 | 3 | 160 |
| 350 | 4 | 180 |
| 375 | 5 | 190 |
| 400 | 6 | 200 |
| 425 | 7 | 220 |
| 450 | 8 | 230 |
| 475 | 9 | 240 |
| 500 | 10 | 260 |

**NOTE:** Reduce the temperature by 20°C (68°F) for fan-assisted ovens.

## APPROXIMATE EQUIVALENTS

1 stick butter = 8 tbs = 4 oz = ½ cup = 115 g

1 cup all-purpose presifted flour = 4.7 oz

1 cup granulated sugar = 8 oz = 220 g

1 cup (firmly packed) brown sugar = 6 oz = 220 g to 230 g

1 cup confectioners' sugar = 4½ oz = 115 g

1 cup honey or syrup = 12 oz

1 cup grated cheese = 4 oz

1 cup dried beans = 6 oz

1 large egg = about 2 oz or about 3 tbs

1 egg yolk = about 1 tbs

1 egg white = about 2 tbs

## LIQUID CONVERSIONS

| U.S. | IMPERIAL | METRIC |
|---|---|---|
| 2 tbs | 1 fl oz | 30 ml |
| 3 tbs | 1½ fl oz | 45 ml |
| ¼ cup | 2 fl oz | 60 ml |
| ⅓ cup | 2½ fl oz | 75 ml |
| ⅓ cup + 1 tbs | 3 fl oz | 90 ml |
| ⅓ cup + 2 tbs | 3½ fl oz | 100 ml |
| ½ cup | 4 fl oz | 125 ml |
| ⅔ cup | 5 fl oz | 150 ml |
| ¾ cup | 6 fl oz | 175 ml |
| ¾ cup + 2 tbs | 7 fl oz | 200 ml |
| 1 cup | 8 fl oz | 250 ml |
| 1 cup + 2 tbs | 9 fl oz | 275 ml |
| 1¼ cups | 10 fl oz | 300 ml |
| 1⅓ cups | 11 fl oz | 325 ml |
| 1½ cups | 12 fl oz | 350 ml |
| 1⅔ cups | 13 fl oz | 375 ml |
| 1¾ cups | 14 fl oz | 400 ml |
| 1¾ cups + 2 tbs | 15 fl oz | 450 ml |
| 2 cups (1 pint) | 16 fl oz | 500 ml |
| 2½ cups | 20 fl oz (1 pint) | 600 ml |
| 3¾ cups | 1½ pints | 900 ml |
| 4 cups | 1¾ pints | 1 liter |

## WEIGHT CONVERSIONS

| U.S./U.K. | METRIC | U.S./U.K. | METRIC |
|---|---|---|---|
| ½ oz | 15 g | 7 oz | 200 g |
| 1 oz | 30 g | 8 oz | 250 g |
| 1½ oz | 45 g | 9 oz | 275 g |
| 2 oz | 60 g | 10 oz | 300 g |
| 2½ oz | 75 g | 11 oz | 325 g |
| 3 oz | 90 g | 12 oz | 350 g |
| 3½ oz | 100 g | 13 oz | 375 g |
| 4 oz | 125 g | 14 oz | 400 g |
| 5 oz | 150 g | 15 oz | 450 g |
| 6 oz | 175 g | 1 lb | 500 g |

# INDEX

## ABOUT THE AUTHOR

**RAQUEL PELZEL**'s work has been featured in *Saveur*, the *Wall Street Journal*, *Every Day with Rachael Ray*, *Shape*, and *Epicurious*, among many others. Formerly an editor at *Cook's Illustrated* and the senior food editor and test kitchen director for Tasting Table, Pelzel has written more than 20 cookbooks and has judged Food Network shows including *Chopped Junior* and *Beat Bobby Flay*. Pelzel lives in Brooklyn, New York, with her two sons.